The Resilient Writer

The Resilient Writer

Tales of Rejection and Triumph from 23 Top Authors

Catherine Wald

A Karen and Michael Braziller Book

PERSEA BOOKS / NEW YORK

Persea Books, Inc.
853 Broadway
New York, New York 10003

Library of Congress Cataloging-in-Publication Data

The resilient writer : tales of rejection and triumph from 23 top authors / Catherine Wald.—1st ed.
p. cm.
"A Karen and Michael Braziller book."
ISBN 0-89255-307-3 (pbk. : alk. paper)
1. Authors, American—20th century—Biography. 2. Authors, and publishers—United States. 3. Literature publishing—United States. 4. Rejection (Psychology) 5. Authorship. I. Wald, Catherine.
PS129.R465 2005
810.9'0054—dc22
2004029080

Designed by Rita Lascaro

Manufactured in the United States of America

First Edition

This book is dedicated to rejected writers everywhere, to the creative spirit that drives our quest to speak and to be heard, and to the pure pigheadedness that keeps us going against all odds.

Contents

Acknowledgments

F IRST, I'D LIKE TO THANK every editor, agent, publisher, employer, teacher, classmate, love interest, friend, and relation who has ever rejected me or my writing. Without them, I could never have come up with the idea for this book.

That *The Resilient Writer* actually saw the light of day is due in great part to my wonderfully supportive and communicative agent, Christina Ward; to my steadfast and visionary publisher, Karen Braziller; and to all those who encouraged this project and my web site, www.rejectioncollection.com, from the get-go—especially Brian Bonini, Joy Cain, Mark Chimsky, Carol Conn, John Delehanty, Arthur Golden, Randy Kraft, Alex Shapiro, Melisse Shapiro, Leslie Shipman, Gerry Vazquez and Jill Vitiello. And bless Connie Baxter and Betty Wald for reading the final manuscript.

Every author interviewed for this book was extremely generous with his or her time, wisdom, and stories; and many of them also helped me connect with other writers. Others who deserve thanks are Oscar Hijuelos, Anne Kyle, Michael Pietsch, Nahid Rachlin, Gail Tsukiyama, and Tony Schwartz.

Finally, I'd like to offer my heartfelt appreciation to Reb, Benjamin, Nina, and other family members for putting up with all my myriad frustrations over the years, and for never, ever rejecting me—even when I was at my crankiest.

Introduction

ONCE UPON A TIME, many rejection slips ago, a bright-eyed college student submitted a sample of his best work to a prestigious professor who led a top-notch creative writing course. He waited. And waited. Finally, he was summoned to the famous writer-in-residence's inner sanctum. There, across a gigantic desk, this larger-than-life personage passed him back his submission, along with her verdict: "Be a banker."

No one could have blamed Chris Bohjalian for chucking it all, right then and there. Instead, he sat down at his desk the next morning and got back to work.

If Bohjalian had taken that professor's judgment to heart, he would never have gone on to write nine novels including a *New York Times* number one bestseller; nor would he have won the New England Book Award or seen his work published in twenty countries around the world.

This book is full of stories like Bohjalian's. If Arthur Golden had crumpled when a high-powered agent told him his manuscript was "too dry," *Memoirs of a Geisha* would have never seen the light of day. If Janet Fitch had thrown her hands up in despair when a writing teacher pointedly suggested that she might do better to write romance novels, she would have never transformed a rejected short story into the bestselling *White Oleander*. If Bob Shacochis had paid heed to the literary agents who advised him to stop writing short stories, he would have never published the American Book Award-winning collection *Easy in the Islands*, which launched his career.

Of course, there was no guarantee that these writers' persistence would pay off. What kept them going when many of us would have given up? What gave them the inner confidence to believe in themselves and their writing, even when the rest of the world was sending them a very different message? Like many other struggling writers, I needed to know the answers to these questions. That's why I wrote this book.

As a nonfiction freelancer for the past twenty-five-plus years, I've had my share of criticisms, disses, and dismissals. But it wasn't until my first novel was rejected by every major publishing house in the civilized Western world that I seriously considered throwing in the towel. The twenty-three authors I interviewed for this book helped me gain the perspective I needed to stop lashing out at friends, family, the publishing industry, and the universe in general—and go back to wrestling with my muses.

Each author has different strategies for dealing with rejection, but they all have come to accept it as part of the territory. Experienced writers know that rejection isn't a hurdle we leap over just once, never to encounter again. It's a constant feature of the writing life, for both the unpublished and the published—and it comes in infinite varieties, from the tiny scrap of paper with a mimeographed "Not for us" to the devastating phone call (or the phone call that never comes) to the indecipherable curl of a lip at a book reading. The sooner we can accept the experience of rejection as an integral component of the writing life, the greater our chances of holding onto our sanity and forging ahead with our creative work.

Experienced writers also know that there is a silver lining to rejection. It can make you a better writer. It can help you lose your fear. It can help you define who you are as an artist and why you're really writing. It can remind you, as Amy Tan says, to "go back to that place where you first wanted to write, or the first moment when you had that epiphany of what writing is about, and try to recapture it." Here are the some of the other lessons I learned in my quest to become a more resilient writer.

We may as well face it: the odds are against us. For every published book or article out there, thousands more have been turned down. Of 150,000 manuscripts submitted to publishers each year only one in three hundred are sold. So if you don't hit it right the first time, it shouldn't come as a total shock.

No one is an instant success. Most authors have at least two or three unpublished novels buried deep inside a closet, attic, or file cabinet. Others deeply regret that their first efforts *were* published.

There is no end to potential insults and injuries. The writers in this book have been sued for libel, lambasted in the national press, and even had deductions nixed by the IRS which told them their writing was a hobby instead of a profession. They've also been cut down to size in countless other ways, both significant and trivial.

Persistence can pay off. More than one of the authors in this book was rejected by every MFA program in the country. Some have collected literally hundreds of rejection slips.

Fame, fortune, and publication aren't cure-alls. You can forget your fantasies that publication will change your life, or even make it easier. Even writers who appear on TV talk shows or win Pulitzer Prizes still have to face the blank computer screen every morning.

Rejection letters don't tell the whole story. Most writers will never know what really went on behind the scenes at the publishing houses that rejected their manuscripts. (And maybe it's better that way!)

Rejection can be energizing. It is possible to use obstacles to spur you on to greater success. Failure can galvanize you to improve your writing, venture into new territory, or reach out directly to your audience.

From painful rejections come powerful lessons. The more accurate a critique, the more it hurts—and the more we can learn from it, if only we can look beyond our bruised egos.

Sometimes what looks like rejection, isn't. Experienced writers understand that a slip that says, "Doesn't work, please try us again," is an expression of interest, not a put-down.

Sometimes the things we fear most never happen. Memoir writers and essayists are understandably nervous about offending friends, family, and readers. More often than not, the tidal wave of outrage they anticipated never materializes. (Then again, occasionally it does.)

Success and failure are equally fluky. Was your short story accepted or rejected by your favorite literary magazine? So much depends upon which graduate student was assigned to skim through the slush pile on that particular day.

Editors are human. Editors are not Olympian gods who make perfect judgments every time. They are just as overwhelmed, disorganized, and subject to whim as other mortals.

If you're looking to make a killing, try another line of work. Only a small minority of authors live off their royalties. Among those who do, seventy-two percent live in shacks in the woods or rent-controlled Manhattan apartments the size of a shoebox.

There is still a market for excellent writing. Authors, editors, and agents all swear that the cream still rises to the top in the publishing world. We must believe this!

You can't judge another writer—or yourself—by one work. Even Flannery O'Connor once said that she would hate to be judged by her first short stories.

The sooner you face up to rejection, the better. Most of us weren't taught to handle rejection in writing classes, workshops, or seminars, but we'd probably be better off if we had been. Start collecting those slips as soon as possible!

You won't always win popularity contests by following your muse. If you are truly guided by your artistic vision, it may lead you where the general public is not willing to follow.

Stop keeping score. Learn to trust the writing process itself. If you do, your finished product is far more likely to succeed.

No one but you can keep you from writing. If you let rejection, despair, or confusion make you quit, that's your choice. You also have the option of choosing to write, no matter what.

Not everyone reading this book is going to become a best-selling author, but we're all capable of becoming resilient writers—writers whose joy in expressing a passion for words, ideas, and stories helps us ride out the inevitable disappointments; writers who take pride in honing our craft; writers who believe in our right to find an audience. This book is meant to urge you forward in living your creative life and reaching your creative goals. The destination isn't guaranteed, but the journey is yours for the taking. Write on!

The Resilient Writer

ELIZABETH BENEDICT

EMMA DODGE HANSON

"Rejections are all in a day's work."

Called "an emotionally profound and richly textured story,"
Elizabeth Benedict's Almost *was named a* New York Times *Notable*
Book and included in Newsweek's *Best Fiction of 2001. Yet when*
the humorous novel was released, the timing couldn't have been
worse: it hit the stores twelve days before the terrorist attacks of
September 11, 2001. How the book rode out the storm is just one of
many unexpected twists in the annals of publishing.

Benedict was born in 1954 in Hartford, Connecticut. She is the
author of Slow Dancing, The Beginner's Book of Dreams, *and*
Safe Conduct. *Her fiction, essays, and reviews have been pub-*
lished in Esquire, Salmagundi, *the* New York Times, *and*
Harper's Bazaar. *She has taught fiction writing at Harvard*
University Extension School, University of Iowa Writers'
Workshop, Princeton University, and the New School, and is also
the author of the acclaimed The Joy of Writing Sex: A Guide for
Fiction Writers.

Q: Almost was your fourth novel. While you were writing it, did you worry less about rejection than you had earlier in your career?
A: During the four years I worked on *Almost*, the publishing industry changed a lot. There was a lot of retrenchment and consolidation, and there were many prolific literary writers who couldn't sell their novels. So I had no assurances the book would be published.

Q: Rejection is always a possibility, whether it's your first novel or your fourth?
A: Yes. Unless you're a Stephen King, or unless your last book was a big bestseller. I don't really separate being rejected from being a writer. It's part of your job. Publishing is a business. What you're trying to do is interest a businessperson in your writing, and the businessperson has to decide whether this is the right article, book, or short story for his or her publication. Part of your job as a writer is to send your work to people who you think will like it.

It's not quite "I was rejected, and therefore I'm not really a writer," or "I was rejected, and therefore something bad happened." People in business make deals, and often the deal you want doesn't happen. That's what getting rejected is. It's not necessarily a definitive comment on you or your talent.

Q: And yet, when writers are first starting out, they don't see it that way.
A: Yes. But rejection is not a stage that you outgrow and get over. Every time you don't see your book in a bookstore, you feel rejected; every time you don't win a prize and somebody else wins a prize, you feel rejected; every time somebody writes a stupid review on Amazon and gives your book one star, you feel rejected. Rejection comes in many forms—but it's part of the process of writing and publishing.

Q: Was it hard to find a publisher for Almost?
A: It involved a large number of rejections. I tried to sell *Almost*

4

when I had one hundred and thirty pages of it, but it was rejected by everybody who saw it. Of course I was disappointed.

But also, once the rejections started piling up, I had a bit of a crisis. I said, "If these people don't respond in the way I intend, I'm doing something wrong here." I had to rethink and re-imagine the book. I recreated the voice. And I rewrote certain chapters at least fifty times.

I also had the good fortune to talk to two of the editors who had said no. They liked what I was doing, but they had some real problems with it. They rejected the manuscript, but they offered to share some of their thoughts with me, and I listened to what they said. I'm not going to listen to everybody, but I *am* going to listen to a smart editor who likes what I'm doing.

Q: Is that kind of interchange unusual?
A: No. Writing is a collaborative process. You do it by yourself, but you get a lot of feedback from people: your agent, your friends, your editors. Editors very rarely accept a book as it's written. There is invariably rewriting that needs to be done.

Q: How do you rewrite one chapter fifty times?
A: *Almost* took me four years to write, and it's two hundred and sixty pages long. But I didn't write half a page a day. I wrote and rewrote and threw away and then rewrote some more.

My work relies heavily on emotional nuance, on slight changes in people's feelings and perceptions, and everything needs to be very finely calibrated in order to work. So the kind of rewriting I do is both on a large scale and a very tiny scale. You can't just bang it out. Once I get the emotional terrain figured out, I then spend a lot of time polishing the prose, the way a sculptor like Brancusi polishes marble.

Q: It sounds like you don't have a problem incorporating feedback into your writing process.
A: No, and I don't think it is a problem for most writers. You

can't do this for twenty years and fall apart every time somebody doesn't like your stuff.

When my first book was published, a friend of mine who was in medical school said, "You're so brave. I couldn't take sending my work out and getting rejected." And I thought, "I couldn't stand one minute in medical school." Getting a short story rejected is hardly dissecting a cadaver or dealing with a bullet wound in the emergency room.

If somebody doesn't like my short story, it certainly stings, but compared with people who risk their lives or save lives or teach underprivileged kids, writing fiction is a very luxurious way to live.

Q: How did you get your first short story published?
A: I wrote a short story more than twenty years ago [about a teenage girl living in New York] and I sent it to the *New Yorker.* Somebody sent a form rejection with a little scribble at the bottom saying, "Sorry." A human being had rejected me! So I kept rewriting this story, and I kept sending it to the *New Yorker.* I ended up having a correspondence with this person.

I sent that story to fifteen places over the years, and everybody sort of liked it, but not enough to publish it. Three years after I had first started sending it out, I woke up one morning and I said, "*Seventeen* magazine!" I sent it there, it was published, and it won a National Magazine Award.

So you have to just keep sending your stuff out. You have to keep rewriting it and listening to what people say. There's nothing organized or predictable about the process. It's not something you can go into with a game plan. You just have to keep doing it.

Because of certain developments in publishing—people selling a first novel for a million dollars and having it made into a movie—many people have an expectation that that's what they can look forward to. It's not. That may be the story for a handful of lucky people, but that's not what a writer's career looks like.

Q: Do you let rejections bother you at all?
A: Oh, sure! They're all annoying and painful. I don't mean to say I'm unfazed by them. But it's all in a day's work, when you look back on it. It's like doctors who get called in the middle of the night. You don't like being called in the middle of the night. You'd rather be sleeping. You'd rather people not be sick. But that's part of your job description. And having people say, "No, I don't want to publish your work," is part of the writer's job.

Q: How did you develop that perspective?
A: I didn't start out with it. But writing is sort of like being in a relationship. You can't just focus on the bad days; you have to look at the bigger picture. Some days your partner is grumpy and hurts your feelings, and it's very painful. But when you look back on it, you can say, "I was having a bad day. My partner was having a bad day. That's life."

Work that gets turned down is just part of the process. I imagine that people who don't like that don't keep doing it. They get a job. I can live with the kind of risks I take as a writer, which is the uncertainty and the financial problems. A lot of people wouldn't want to live the way I live. Sometimes *I* don't want to live this way!

Q: So why do you keep going?
A: Writing suits my interests. I hope it suits my talents, but it suits my temperament in a serious way. My idea of a great way to spend my time is to stay home in my pajamas writing and to not see anyone for days on end. That's not everybody's idea of a great time or a great life.

It's very hard to live with the financial uncertainty. You have to learn ways to support yourself, whether it's through journalism or teaching or writing annual reports for big corporations. I have fiction writer friends who continue to do those things even after they've written best-selling novels.

Q: Sophy, the main character in Almost, *is a struggling writer. I loved the scene where she suddenly decides she can't stand a novel she's working on. Is that based on your own experience?*
A: I never wrote a book about Lili Boulanger. But I did write a hundred pages of a novel that I gave up on. I've written a few things that I've given up on. I haven't experienced anything as dramatic as what Sophy goes through in the book, but there is a certain point where you say, "This isn't going anywhere."

Writers are obsessive. We're all obsessed about different things. But you can't do this unless you're slightly mad, like a dog that won't let go of a sock in his mouth.

The novels that I've written have all come from something powerful in me that I wanted to work though. There has to be something that I'm working out emotionally. If it lacks that kind of pull for me, I can't keep going. And if my emotional attachment to the subject is strong enough, it overcomes my feelings of uncertainty.

Q: What about Sophy's ambivalence about taking high-paying work-for-hire writing? Is that something that figures into your life?
A: Sure. I'm grateful for the high-paying hack work, and I usually wish there were more of it. I had the good fortune to write a column once a month for two years for Japanese *Playboy*, and I made more money than I ever have. Unfortunately, that gig is long gone and nothing has come along to replace it.

Q: In your work as a teacher, do you find that you're called upon to advise your students about rejection?
A: I think the question of rejection isn't separate from the question of self-doubt that goes with your life as a writer. I don't give them chats about rejection, but I do talk about how you keep going when you feel all this self-doubt.

Q: What's the answer?
A: The answer is that you just keep going. It really is like being

an athlete. Athletes don't compete in Olympics because they got up one morning and said, "I think I'd like to be in the Olympics tomorrow." They spend their lives working on it and training and doing what they need to do to get there.

In my writing classes I ask the students to talk about self-doubt, and I tell them my own stories of work getting rejected and constant feelings of anxiety and insecurity. All writers have those feelings. Or I should say, I haven't come across any who don't.

Once you're published, you don't stop getting rejected. You get different kinds of rejection, and you have to deal with that. It's very hard when you have a book published that doesn't get reviewed and doesn't take off. Or it does get reviewed in the *New York Times* and *still* doesn't take off. That's rejection too.

Sometimes there are rejections that aren't personal. For example, *Almost* came out twelve days before September 11th. It was the lead review in the *New York Times* on September 9th, and I had several interviews scheduled for the week of September 11th. Much of that got derailed. And I was certain the book was finished, that interest in it would never pick up.

Q: But eventually the book did very well.
A: It turned out that the book had an interesting life after September 11th. Because it's about a sudden death, a lot of reviewers discussed it in light of the 9/11 attacks. The book was published in paperback the following spring with a beautiful summer cover, and it became very successful as a paperback— which was a great surprise, after its inauspicious beginning.

Q: When your first novel was published, you were worried about how your family was going to react.
A: Actually, I worried about that with all the books.

Q: Did your fears turn out to be unfounded?
A: My grandmother didn't like my first book because it had sex

in it. But the rest of my family has been very supportive, even when I've exploited them and told all the family secrets.

Q: *Did your book on writing about sex open you up to a lot of criticism and rejection?*
A: Only one reviewer, Jonathan Franzen, was undone by the book. His attack was published in *The New Yorker*. But his vitriol was much more about his paranoia than it was about the book, and the ways in which he misread my book were stunning. Since *The Joy of Writing Sex* was first published, it's become something of a classic on writing fiction, and it's taught in all sorts of distinguished schools.

As far as my opening myself up to criticism and rejection— the book isn't about *my* sex life. It's about writing about sex in fiction, and if people don't like my ideas on how to write a good sex scene—well, I'm not crushed by that. I've revealed far more of myself in my fiction than in *The Joy of Writing Sex*.

We get sidetracked by thinking that sex is the most revealing thing we can write about. Writing about loneliness, abandonment, or an unhappy marriage can be more revealing than writing about sex.

Q: *Does using humor in your work open you more up to rejection?*
A: I'm sure it does. Some people don't like my sense of humor. One of the reviews of *Almost* said I was a funny person, even though she didn't like my jokes. That was infuriating! I've given readings from *Almost* where people howled with laughter, and then I've read the same material to a different group and heard dead silence. I sometimes want to stop and say, "Other people think this is really funny. What's wrong with you?"

Obviously some readers and reviewers don't get my humor or my sensibility. In a review of *Almost* in the *New York Times*, a critic said I was "almost" a very good writer.

Q: Oh, no!

A: That was painful. Nobody's *not* hurt by that kind of rejection, but you have to have the sturdiness—and maybe the arrogance—to say, "My expression of my feelings, my assertion of my view of the world, is more important than this rejection."

Q: You once said, "Writing is an act of courage that writers either need to have or need to acquire."

A: Writing is a complicated act—of courage, stamina, renunciation, rewriting, isolation, uncertainty—as well as those moments that sometimes stretch into days of enormous satisfaction and intense pleasure.

C. WALD

MARY KAY BLAKELY

"When I don't get any negative feedback,
I think I'm not really doing my job."

*Mary Kay Blakely's courage in speaking against prevailing cultural
trends has both won her acclaim and landed her in hot water. But
despite the ups and downs of her writing life, the longtime activist
and journalism professor continues to believe that writers are
important agents of change in society—and she puts her money
where her mouth is.*

*Born in Chicago in 1948, Blakeley became a feminist, activist,
and journalist in the mid-1970s. She began her writing career as a
columnist for the* Fort Wayne Journal-Gazette. *A contributing editor to* Ms. *magazine since 1981, she has written about social and
political issues for publications such as the* New York Times, *the*
Los Angeles Times, Time, Parents, Vogue, *and* Mirabella. *She is
the author of three memoirs,* Wake Me When It's Over; American
Mom: Motherhood, Politics and Humble Pie; *and* Red, White
and Oh, So Blue: Memoir of A Political Depression.

Blakely, an associate professor at the Missouri School of

Journalism, was one of the plaintiffs in a lawsuit on behalf of the rights of freelance writers, Tasini v. The New York Times, *which the Supreme Court decided in the plaintiffs' favor in 2001. She is the mother of two grown sons and divides her time between New York City and Columbia, Missouri.*

Q: *You landed your first journalism job as a result of your involvement in the women's movement. How did your work as a feminist influence your writing?*

A: Being active in the women's movement in the late sixties and early seventies was really good training for being a writer because people rejected you all the time. It's hard to recreate those times now. There was hostility on every front about almost every single idea we were talking about. We were all labeled "libbers," which meant, "You don't have to pay attention to them." And I used to think, "Wait a minute—motherhood, discrimination, jobs—we're talking about your mother, your wife, your sister, your daughter!"

I didn't have journalism training, but I did know that if you told a story, people would relate to it, as long as it was interesting or compelling. If you could find the area in which the reader was least threatened and then expand on it *after* they'd agreed with you, you could win them over.

This all goes back to rejection. It can be useful to find out, why aren't my ideas getting across? That doesn't mean I have to change my ideas, but I either have to find a different way or a different place to express them. If the only alternative is to be quiet, or to not have an audience, then it does pressure you into widening your own definition of what you can do.

Q: *How did you break into national publications after writing for the local Fort Wayne, Indiana, newspaper?*

A: If I didn't get a huge boost from my editor at *The Journal-Gazette*, I might never have had the persistence to keep going at national magazines, because I got rejection after rejection. When you get a rejection, you can't help thinking, "What did I do wrong?" or, "What's wrong with me?"

After my editor wrote to the *New York Times* about me, they ran an exceptionally long series of my work in the "Hers" column. That column was read by every editor of every women's magazine. The irony is that, all of a sudden, I got calls from editors who had sent me form rejection letters.

That's when I learned it's not always what you've done, or what you're actually saying. It's all about access. The same idea that has no cachet coming from someone editors don't know, has lots coming from someone they do know.

Q: You've said that women are published far less often than men. It's hard to believe that's still true in the twenty-first century.
A: After September 11, 2001, journalist Geneva Overholser counted the Op Ed pieces in the *New York Times* and the *Washington Post*. Of sixty-five pieces, *four* were by women. But is war only a guys' topic? Aren't women citizens? It's not that we write less, or that there are fewer female writers; we just don't get those prime spots, and we don't get fifty percent by any stretch of the imagination.

Q: Do writers ever have to hide their beliefs in order to get published?
A: My feeling is you should never, never compromise what you have to say; but you *can* keep searching for a different way to say it.

If mainly right-wing conservatives are being published, do you turn yourself into one? No, not ever. But we have to learn how to set our large ideas into a shorter format. Life has speeded up so much, and we have to acknowledge this. We all have room to be that kind of versatile, and I think we can do it without compromising what we think.

Q: What advice do you give to students who want to pursue journalism as a career?

A: I always say, "Don't quit the day job." But I also feel passion-ately that writing and journalism have never been more impor-tant. Writers have to up the level of discourse in the culture. What we've got in the media today is a culture of spins. We're fighting for journalism versus public relations. People are feeling empty about politics, but they don't know how to combat it. They feel like they're eating a diet with no substance, and the media give so little to stimulate their thinking!

Q: How do you keep going in the face of such odds?
A: The incredibly talented and thoughtful young people in my journalism classes are a cure for burnout.

Also I feel that the pendulum has to swing back again some-how. We are a capitalist culture, and so much is about sales and marketing. But we also have the Internet and the alternative press in this country, especially since 9/11. You can't make a liv-ing writing for the electronic media, but they are at least open-ing up space for ideas.

Q: Do you encourage your students to write for alternative publi-cations?
A: Yes, because you can at least have an audience. I tell them not to stop submitting their work to print magazines—but in the meantime, getting published anywhere helps erase the feeling of "I'm useless, why bother?"

Q: You're a good example of a writer who keeps going whatever the obstacles. Why haven't you given up?
A: There could be a frightening answer to that: Because I'm stubborn, and I won't take no for an answer. But I also absolutely believe that writers are vital to civilization. We're the ones who come up with different ways of seeing and knowing. We're the ones who process ideas and put them out there for people who are too busy, people who run banks or grocery sto-ries or gas stations.

It's important for writers to believe that we are agents of change, even if we may not see the results in our own lifetimes. Look at history. Harriet Beecher Stowe's *Uncle Tom's Cabin* was a very flawed piece of literature, but she had a huge impact on her times. So did Harper Lee's *To Kill a Mockingbird* and Marilyn French's *The Women's Room*. We may feel powerless, but we're not. We really can change things.

Q: You often encourage writers to form support groups. Why is that?
A: I think I came to that intuitively, because writing is such a solo endeavor. It's a terrible job for an extrovert! You have to have allies—readers, writers, or editors. You need to know you're not alone in this world.

Q: Getting a response from other writers and from readers has always been important to you.
A: I learned that early on, when writing for the newspaper in Fort Wayne. It was the letters to the editor that kept stimulating my own thinking. Readers have always kept me alive, even though I wasn't always writing the majority point of view. They made editors feel that what I was saying was important.

When I don't get any negative feedback, I think I'm not really doing my job, because I'm not making anybody mad.

Q: Sometimes writers with vision are so far ahead of the curve that they can't get published. Has this ever happened to you?
A: A perfect example is my book *Red, White and Oh, So Blue*. I began writing it in 1994, and that book proposal was rejected seventeen times. It was kind of heartbreaking for my agent, because *American Mom* had just come out, to great reviews. When we told publishers that the next book was about political depression, they'd say, "What is she talking about? The economy is booming! We just won the Cold War!" But I was depressed because I was looking at things like the collapse of social services and the image America had among other countries.

Writers often get ahead of the culture. When we do, rejection becomes a reality. By the time I wrote that book, I had published hundreds of magazine pieces, and I was not unfamiliar to editors. But it didn't matter. I was out of sync with the culture.

Q: Did your experience with Red White and Oh, So Blue *cause you to doubt yourself?*
A: It did. But I also understood by that time that publishing is about marketing and the flow of money, and whether a particular piece of writing will make a profit. Most publishing institutions are not particularly on a mission to change the world. The first issue is the bottom line.

It really looked as if I wasn't going to be able to get that book published because the whole culture was in a "Don't worry, be happy" mode. Greed is the major theme in the book, and it's still a major theme in the culture. A lot more people are writing about it now. But when we were trying to sell it in 1994, publishers would say, "What other book is it like?" When I couldn't come up with an answer, I had to think, "Maybe I am wrong." It did cause some periods of real doubt. But it wasn't really courageous to keep going.

Q: No?
A: No, it wasn't. Because the truth is, I couldn't write about anything else, anyway. I was obsessed with this idea. I was just intent on getting it out of my craw.

Q: Writing a book that doesn't make money is still better than being obsessed and not writing a book?
A: Exactly! I look back on that book now and see that it was very imperfect. It could have been so much better than it was. But it did allow me to move on. I'm not unhappy that I published it.

Q: Telling people things they don't want to hear is risky. What makes you a good risk-taker?

A: I don't think it's because I have courage. I think it's because I don't see any other way to do it. And because I don't think about the consequences, which might not be a bad trait to acquire with age.

When I'm writing, I'm not ever thinking, "Will so-and-so like this?" I'm *completely* obsessed with, "Is this right? Is this the way I meant to say it?" I really only become aware of the risk later, when the writing's done.

Q: *Speaking of risk, the passages in which you unveil your deepest, darkest secrets have often been the ones that got the most positive response from readers.*
A: When you have a compromising moment in your life, you worry that other people are going to find out about it. But in fact, if you come out and honestly say, "This is what I did, and this is how it happened," most people are more likely to identify with you than to judge you. I just have seen that over and over.

Q: *You were one of eleven plaintiffs who sued the* New York Times *for publishing freelance writers' work on the Internet without permission. After the Supreme Court ruled against the* Times, *a leaked internal memo apparently revealed that the* Times' *legal counsel had instructed its editors not to hire any of the plaintiffs. Was that the worst rejection of your life?*
A: In a lot of ways it was the most hurtful. In that case I couldn't even say, "I must have been wrong," because even the Supreme Court voted 7-2 in our favor.

It was explicitly clear that the reason I could no longer write for the *Times* had nothing to do with my editors or their assessment of my work; it had only to do with the lawyers of the *New York Times.* What is kind of heartbreaking is that the restriction is not only from the *New York Times* but from other defendants, including Time Warner, which owns about fifteen magazines.

Q: Before that, you'd had a long and positive relationship with the Times.

A: The real irony for me is that Supreme Court Justice Ruth Bader Ginsburg based her decision in *Tasini v. The New York Times* on one of my essays, "Remembering Jane," which told part of the history of the abortion rights struggle, using the increasing violence against abortion clinics in Indiana as an example.

When that essay first came in to the *Times,* they were so deluged with faxes from anti-abortion groups that they had to disconnect the fax. There were threats and pickets, and the *Times* really *did* have to worry about harm to their property and their staff. It was truly extraordinary that the *Times* decided not to be intimidated by threats and to run the piece. Then, ten years later, that same piece got me banned.

I know this ban will eventually be lifted, and it's probably my job in the meantime to keep publishing in other venues so my work doesn't become irrelevant. But was it leveling? It absolutely was.

Q: Speaking of leveling, what's the worst review you ever got?

A: I vividly remember the first review of my very first book, *Wake Me When It's Over*, in *Mother Jones.* It was by Susan Faludi, who hadn't yet published *Backlash.* The review was such an incredible trash of my book! I didn't even know this could *happen* to a person. And then, of course, *Backlash* came out and became a bestseller.

Q: What did Susan Faludi have against your book?

A: What made her so mad was the cover copy on the galley. The publisher had decided my book was "the memoir of a working supermom." While Faludi was writing her review, I was telling Random House, "You've got to take that word *supermom* off the publicity, because it trivializes a hugely important issue. It's a put-down of the very audience that you're trying to reach." And so, they did; "supermom" never appeared on the book. But it set the way Faludi read it, and for her, there was nothing redeeming about the whole entire book.

Q: After Backlash *was published, a mutual friend insisted on getting you two together.*
A: She did, and by the time we had lunch, it was much harder for Faludi than it was for me. She felt just mortified, and she couldn't believe that she had so misunderstood me.

So maybe there's a flip side to rejection. Her review reminded me that you can attack the enemy, but you can never get mean and personal about it. Another way of understanding rejection is that if it's proven wrong, it's harder for the person who issued the bad review than it is for the person who got caught in the crosshairs.

Q: How do you feel when you get rejection letters?
A: My first response is overwhelming disappointment. There have been times when I've felt embarrassed because I didn't represent the idea right, or because there's somebody out there who thinks I'm stupid. But, as I say to students all the time, you have to get over those feelings early on if you're going to be a writer.

Being a writer is a perpetually humbling experience. Every day you have to be willing to confront your own stupidity. You have to be willing to say, "Oh, man, that was a stupid sentence. It's not as brilliant as I thought it would be when it was floating around in my head." You get to experience shame and humiliation in all kinds of different ways.

Q: But that doesn't stop you.
A: No, it *can't.* It's part of the job.

CHRIS BOHJALIAN

VICTORIA BLEWER

"I think it was at around rejection
two-hundred-and-fifty that I began to wonder
if I was ever going to sell anything."

*Chris Bohjalian collected 250 rejection slips before he finally sold a
short story. He calls his first published novel,* A Killing in the Real
World, *"the single worst first novel ever published, bar none." But
Bohjalian never let self-doubt, criticism, or disapproval keep him
from writing. If he had, he would have never gone on to write the
novel* Midwives, *which was named one of the best books of the year
by* Publisher's Weekly, *and rose to number one on the* New York
Times *bestseller list.*

*Bohjalian was born in White Plains, New York, in 1960 and now
lives in Lincoln, Vermont, with his wife and daughter. His other novels include* Water Witches, Trans-Sister Radio, *and* The Buffalo
Soldier. *His work has been translated into seventeen languages and
published in twenty countries. A columnist for the* Burlington Free
Press *since 1992, he has also written for* Cosmopolitan, Reader's
Digest, *the* Boston Globe Sunday Magazine, *and others. A collection of his essays,* Idyll Banter, *was published in 2003.*

Q: You had a truly horrendous rejection when you were young. Can you tell me about that?

A: When I was a sophomore at Amherst College, I wanted desperately to take a creative writing course with the writer-in-residence, a terrific novelist whose work I cherished. The course was limited, and each student had to submit a sample story to see if he or she was worthy to be among the anointed.

I submitted my story, and a few weeks later I was summoned to the writer's office in the great brick monolith that housed the English Department. The writer-in-residence slid my story across a desk that seemed to me then to be the size of a putting green. She said, "Chris—and I don't need to know how to pronounce your last name—I have three words for you: Be a banker."

Q: What did you do? What did you say?

A: I said, "Thank you." I tried to suck it up; I doubt I lost my composure. But I did allow myself to beat a very hasty retreat, and I avoided her office and that hallway for the duration of college.

I can remember lumbering off, despairing, in slow motion. It was January, and it was five o'clock in the afternoon. It was pitch dark and cold, and I was living in a hideous fraternity with no heat. I was devastated, but not daunted. I got back on the horse the next day.

Q: When a professor or editor tells a budding writer to give up, most people take them at their word. Why didn't you?

A: Because the actual process of writing has always given me pleasure. After I had been told to be a banker, I wrote a couple of short stories and massive amounts for the college newspaper. However I never did take any creative writing courses after that, nor did I even *consider* getting an MFA. There may be a connection.

Q: Have you forgiven this unnamed writer-in-residence?

A: No. In my opinion, it is a professional editor's job to reject young writers and say the cruel things that need to be said. It is not the role of a creative writing professor to devastate young people.

Q: *And yet you still admire this person's work?*
A: Yes. The world is filled with immensely gifted novelists whose work I respect and enjoy but who I wouldn't want to have lunch with.

Q: *Is it true that you collected two-hundred-fifty rejection slips in the beginning of your career?*
A: Yes, I did! That was in 1984, when I was twenty-three years old. I have rejection slips from the literary quarterlies and from every mainstream magazine that was publishing fiction. They were a veritable *Who's Who* of editors in the early 1980s, from *Redbook* and *Ladies' Home Journal* and *Cosmopolitan* and the *New Yorker* and *Harper's*, as well as *The Sewanee Review* and so forth.

When you amass a lot of rejections, you begin to prioritize them. First there's the three-by-five-inch card that's simply signed "The Editors." Then there's the one- or two-sentence note on the editor's stationery that's paper-clipped to the story. Finally there's the Pulitzer Prize of rejection slips, the three- or four-paragraph response in which the editor has not merely read your story, but she's offered a critique. Those letters end with that wonderful carrot, "Please try us again."

The scary thing is, how you cling to those strange bits of wood when the ship is sinking. I would savor, for example, a letter from Cullen Murphy of the *Atlantic* because it was from him, and because it said something encouraging. I didn't take as much pride, to be perfectly honest, in encouraging notes from somebody who was obviously a twenty-three-year-old assistant editor.

At some point, you go from taking pride that you're sending material out, to fear. At around number two hundred fifty, I began to stop taking pride in this wall of rejections that I had built, and I began to wonder if I was ever going to sell anything.

I decided that I needed to approach this from a more practical vantage point, so I read two or three months of *Cosmopolitan*, which then was publishing a lot of fiction. Then I wrote a story called "Sparks," about a young female fashion model whose relationship with her ad executive husband is starting to deteriorate, and I set it on Fire Island. It's got a lot of beach volleyball with scantily clad young people, and it sold to *Cosmopolitan* in 1984. I was thrilled.

Q: How do you feel about that story today?
A: In hindsight, I think it's a pretty adequate short story for a twenty-four-year-old. On the other hand, if I ever decide to publish my short stories in a collection, "Sparks" won't be in it.

Q: Did you really hang all your rejections on the wall in those days?
A: Yes. It wasn't just one wall. It ran around two parts of two walls, between the bookshelves and into the bathroom of my boyhood home, because after college I lived at home for a year.

Q: What did your parents make of all this?
A: I had wonderfully supportive parents, but I did have other relatives telling me, that first year, that it was time to pack it in. I also had friends who were worried about my stability.

Q: What did the sale of "Sparks" do for you? Besides financially, which I'm sure wasn't much.
A: It gave me the confidence to embark upon a novel. I had two conflicting notions. The first was, maybe I should try to parlay this into more short stories. But then I realized how many stabs it had taken to sell one story. And I'd always enjoyed novels more than short stories—especially big, sprawling multigenerational family sagas. So, once I'd sold a short story, I decided to embark upon a novel.

Q: It's amazing, isn't it, how little encouragement it takes to keep us going?

A: Yup! I didn't write another short story for two years after that. Instead, I wrote what became the single worst first novel ever published, bar none: *A Killing in the Real World*.

I was once signing books at a bookstore in Denver. Afterward, I met a collector with a Mylar-covered edition of *A Killing in the Real World*. I felt so terrible when he told me what he had spent to buy that copy that I insisted on paying for his copy of *The Buffalo Soldier*.

Q: How did A Killing in the Real World *get to be that bad?*

A: I wrote a novel about four graduates of a women's college who are brought together in New York City when one of their group dies. I envisioned it as a coming-of-age novel about people in the 1980s.

But the editor who wanted to acquire it at St. Martin's suggested that I rewrite it with more of a "mystery flair." The reality that I was *this* close to selling a novel caused me to transform my coming-of-age novel into a vapid, violent, predictable murder mystery.

Q: So first Cosmo, *and then St. Martin's . . .*

A: Do you see a pattern here? I think I developed a spine after that first novel. It took the reality of reading my first novel between hard covers to understand that I needed to be focused on stories that I cared passionately about, and not write based on the commercial demands of the marketplace.

Q: That's a really tough line to walk, isn't it?

A: It is, but here's the truth: I have always been most successful when I write about subjects that are so esoteric and Byzantine that no editor should want to go near them. For example, when I said I wanted to write a novel about a midwife on trial for manslaughter, somebody told me, "No one is interested in midwifery." When I was writing a book about a transsexual lesbian, I was surrounded by people who were telling me not to go there. Fortunately, for the last ten years, I've had an editor who has been very supportive—whether I want to write about midwives, transsexual lesbians, or homeopaths.

Q: Even in "today's financially conservative publishing environment"?
A: Yes. People are so concerned with the consolidation of publishing. They say that big commercial houses are reluctant to publish risky fiction. But that has never been my experience, no matter how obscure or risky the subject matter of my fiction.

Q: Why do you think that is?
A: I have a terrific champion of an editor. And then, I've always been fortunate to work with people in publishing who still care about books, not just as commerce, but as passionate totems of our existence.

Q: So your success as a writer has to do with staying true to your passion?
A: Yes. One of the things I always tell young writers as they embark upon a novel, is, "Don't necessarily write about what you know, and don't necessarily write about what you don't know. Write about a subject that you care so desperately about that you're willing to get up every day at five a.m. and write about it." If you're that interested in the subject matter, you've got a much better chance of writing a book that's intriguing and surprising and will cause people to turn the pages with rapt fascination.

Q: Looking back on your "worst first novel ever published," do you wish you had told the editor, "I'm not interested in writing a mystery, forget it?"
A: Yes! I should never have agreed to even *try* and write a mystery. It's not what I do. It's not what I care about.

Q: What if you hadn't rewritten it? What kind of book would it have been?

A: Instead of being the single worst published novel, bar none, it would have been a perfectly adequate first effort with all the flaws that permeate most first novels. Every novelist's first or second, or even third novel is an apprentice work that should probably never be published. It's the same way that a concert pianist never goes directly to Carnegie Hall; you've got years and years of practice first.

I don't think my second or third novels are hideous. But I really don't think it was until I wrote my fourth novel, *Water Witches,* that I really started to understand how to move a plot forward, how to be with my characters, and how to make their inner lives interesting for readers.

As a culture, we love those Cinderella stories that mark the successful first novel, like Zadie Smith's *White Teeth* and Donna Tartt's *The Secret History.* But the truth is that most of us *aren't* Zadie Smith and Donna Tartt. It takes us a few novels to get it right.

Q: When you look back on your first three novels, how do you feel?

A: I'm not unhappy that my second and third novels sold. But I also do not allow my first, second or third novels to be put back into print. Nor will I ever.

Q: Midwives *was your first big success. How did the book do before it was touched by Oprah's magic wand in 1998?*

A: It wasn't a monumental bestseller, but it had sold one hundred thousand copies in paperback even before it became a part of Oprah's Book Club. To put a sense of the magnitude of that book club and what a great gift and blessing it was for writers: *Midwives* was a bestseller in its eighth printing prior to being a part of Oprah's Book Club. The other day, I saw that it's in its forty-ninth printing.

Q: What kind of feedback did you get from readers who are midwives?

A: When the book was first published in 1997, I thought they would love it, because it's a story about a gifted midwife belea-guered by a medical and legal community beyond her ken. But when it first came out, a lot of midwives thought I was the Antichrist. Later they understood that it was not about an incompetent midwife, but rather about an immensely compe-tent midwife under siege.

Q: *Did you write that book with a pro-midwife agenda?*
A: No. A lot of people assume I write with a particular agenda. But I never write a book because of an opinion I have on an issue. Rather, I choose issues that have great conflict and great opportunity for human transformation. Those are the two points on a compass that matter most in fiction. I'm just crib-bing from John Gardner when I say that.

Q: *Does rejection play a different role in your life now than it did when you were first getting started?*
A: When I was first getting started, rejection wasn't simply a bar-rier to success; it was a barrier to the profession I wanted to enter. Now I don't worry about whether I'm going to sell a novel or an essay or a short story, but I do worry about how it will be received by readers.

Q: *You say readers, not critics.*
A: I worry about critics, too. But those are two different issues. When I'm writing a book, I'm not thinking about critics. I start worrying about critics when the galleys are going out.

Q: *Are you one of these people who won't read criticism of your work?*
A: No, and I don't believe there are many writers in this world who honestly do not read all their reviews. We all read them. And here's the other dirty little secret: We remember them. Not the good ones, but we remember the bad ones.

The vast majority of the reviews I received are glowing and

thoughtful and laudatory. However, the ones I remember are the ones where the critic clearly didn't understand the book, or disagreed with it, or said my writing was graceless.

I'm always shocked when I get that first copy of the paperback from my publisher and there's all this love from critics on the cover and the back and the first four pages. I have to remind myself, "Oh, yeah, *USA Today* loved that book, the *San Francisco Chronicle* loved that book." Because all I remember is that the *New York Daily News* hated it.

Q: That seems to be a common human trait. We remember the negative more clearly than the positive. How do you deal with that?
A: I remind myself that it's one bad review, and the vast majority have been terrific. Underneath that reasonable façade, however, is that evil little person in the back of your brain who's whispering, "You're a loser. You're a fraud. You'll never sell another manuscript as long as you live." And of course the reality is, this little voice is based upon a review in a newspaper with a circulation of thirty thousand, only three hundred of whom ever bother to read the book page.

Q: Is it true that you once wrote a hundred and twenty pages of a novel and threw it away?
A: Actually, I've done that twice. It was pretty clear to me in both of those cases that the book was not giving me sufficient pleasure to proceed. And while I'm probably strong-willed enough to finish any novel I start, the end product was not going to justify the time.

Q: So that's your yardstick, the pleasure the work is giving you?
A: Yes. Not because I'm selfish and self-absorbed, though I probably am, but because I have learned the hard way that my best books are the ones that give me the greatest pleasure when I'm immersed in them.

Q: It sounds as if you have a good grip on how to deal with rejection. Are there other obstacles that you find more daunting?
A: The biggest obstacles, more times than not, are my own limitations as a writer. I've read novels in which every sentence will give me an inferiority complex. I've read books with paragraphs better than anything I have ever written. This doesn't take the wind out of me sufficiently to prevent me from getting up to write in the morning. But occasionally I will find myself just wishing I was better.

Q: If you had never been published, would you still be writing now?
A: Yes. Because I'm a man of relentless optimism. And because writing itself gives me enough satisfaction. Even as a novelist who is relatively prolific, I still go at least nine to twelve months without a whole lot of human contact about my work. And I think that means you have to derive satisfaction from a well-crafted sentence. You have to enjoy being submerged in your story.

There's nothing in this world, other than hanging around with my wife or my daughter, that gives me more pleasure than writing fiction.

Q: You write a weekly column for The Burlington Free Press. *Does that make up for some of that isolation and lack of feedback involved in novel-writing?*
A: I've been writing that column every single Sunday for twelve or thirteen years now. It's very different from my fiction—it's less dark, more irreverent, and infinitely more personal. I do get a lot of feedback, the vast majority of it gloriously positive. I don't get rejection as a result of the column, but I certainly get people who disagree. Especially since I'm not shy about my opinions.

Q: Disagreeing with your opinion is less of a rejection than getting no response at all.
A: That's absolutely true. I don't go out of my way to offend

people in my column any more than I want to offend people in my fiction, but if I cause them to question themselves or to question me, I'm thrilled.

Q: Is there anything else that you tell writers about rejection?
A: I remind them that they should just view it as their apprenticeship. If the writing is giving them satisfaction, there's no need to stop.

JAMES J. KRIEGSMAN, JR.

WESLEY BROWN

"No one decides that we should
answer the call of the muse. If you answer
the call, that's your responsibility."

*Playwright and novelist Wesley Brown has never been afraid to put
either his artistic or his political convictions on the line—and this
has led to all kinds of rejection. His refusal to be inducted into the
Army in 1968 during the Vietnam War led to an eighteen-month jail
sentence. He described this experience in his first novel,* Tragic
Magic, *which led James Baldwin to call him "a hell of a writer" and
"astoundingly honest." Brown's second novel,* Darktown Strutters,
*which deals with the emotionally charged history of black-faced
minstrelsy in the mid-nineteenth century, was called "original and
visionary" by Ted Solotaroff.*

*Wesley Brown was born in New York City in 1945. He received a
master's degree in literature and creative writing from City College,
where he studied with Susan Sontag and Donald Barthelme. In
addition to his novels, he is the author of four plays and numerous
stories and essays. Brown teaches drama and literature at Rutgers
University, and lives in Columbia County, New York.*

Q: *What role does rejection play in your career as a writer?*
A: Well, it's integral. It's a persistent experience, I think, for most writers. I don't see that the experience of rejection as a creative writer is any different from the experience that most human beings have. One of the central aspects of being alive is not getting what you want.

Q: *What were your earliest rejections as a writer?*
A: The first stories and poems that I sent to magazines of various kinds were all rejected. It started early, and it was something that didn't surprise me. I didn't expect that my work, at that early stage, was going to receive universal acceptance.

Over the years, I've come to believe that something I work on with a great degree of concentration and effort is eventually going to find its way to a readership in one form or another. Sometimes it takes longer than other times, and rejection is part of what one has to go through.

I don't take rejection as a judgment about the value of my work. I just see it as an assessment that an editor or a publisher has made about what was submitted.

Q: *Why weren't you surprised by your early rejections? Did something in your education as a writer lead you to expect them?*
A: I guess it was my education as a human being. I think if you grow up in a family and you engage in the world that is outside your immediate surroundings, you're going to experience obstacles. There are going to be things you do that people are not necessarily going to like. I didn't feel I was done any great injustice as a result of not having my work published on those first tries. It seemed to me to conform to many of the experiences I had growing up and facing obstacles to my will.

Whatever you've written is a public gesture, and it is subject to judgment. You can't assume that those judgments are always going to be favorable. That doesn't necessarily say anything significant about the value of what you've done; it just expresses an opinion of someone else that you can take, use, or discard.

Q: *With such a philosophical attitude, have you ever found your-self getting angry or emotional about a rejection?*
A: Well, you are always disappointed if you've worked very hard on something and it is not accepted. You're not going to be thrilled about that. But I think that if you're a writer, you write for yourself first. It's not that you don't want approval or accept-ance from the world at large. But the impetus for writing shouldn't be driven by acceptance from others.

My impetus for writing has always been to gain clarity about things that are a source of conflict for me. If you are fortunate enough to make a gesture to a world larger than your own imag-ination, you hope there will be some recognition for your effort. But there's no guarantee.

Q: *Tell me about your first novel,* Tragic Magic. *Did you have a hard time getting it published?*
A: I was in a workshop with Susan Sontag at the creative writing program at City College. She liked my work, and she showed a chapter to Ted Solotaroff, who was an editor at Bantam Books, and he sold the hardcover rights to Random House.

I was quite fortunate to catch lightning in a bottle, having an advocate such as Susan Sontag who liked my work, and who was in a position to say to someone like Ted Solotaroff, "Here's some-thing I think you should read." And because he knows and respects her, he reads my manuscript rather than the thirty other things that are on his desk.

When you have that kind of convergence, it's a very fortu-nate position to be in. It's easier than sending your submis-sions to people who don't know who you are. Although you also have to also be *ready* to be lucky. There does come a moment of decision when what you've done has to be judged on its own merits.

Q: *Was* Tragic Magic *a success?*
A: It got favorable reviews in the *New York Times* and in the Chicago, Dallas, and Los Angeles papers. But it didn't sell that well. One reason was that it was published in October of 1978, when there was a newspaper strike in New York. The review in the *Times* did not appear until after the strike ended in February, and a lot of sales were lost because of the delay.

Q: *When* Tragic Magic *came out, did you have dreams of a number one bestseller? After all, you had the imprimatur of James Baldwin, a real master.*
A: I was pleased that the book was well received, but I really had no idea what would happen beyond that. I remembered Grace Paley once said that usually the only thing that comes with publication is silence. So I wasn't thinking in those terms.

Of course we all have fantasies. You allow yourself to go with them for a while, until they run their course, and then you say, "Okay, enough."

Things like being on the *Today* show are rare. For most writers, just being able to feel that you've written the best book you could write, that it was published by people who believed in it, and that there is a possibility of it getting into the hands of an audience, is enough.

Q: *What was your experience getting your second novel published?*
A: *Darktown Strutters* was much more arduous in terms of the number of rejections it received. Finally Steve Schrader, who had an imprint called Cane Hill Press, read the manuscript and said, "I really like a lot of this, but it needs some work. Revise it and give it back to me. If I like it, I'll publish it. If I don't, you won't have to return the advance."

I hadn't had any better offers than that. So that's how *Darktown Strutters* made its publication journey. I had been working on the book since the late seventies, and it was finally published in 1994. And while the journey to publication for

Darktown Strutters was hard, it sold much better than *Tragic Magic.*

Q: *What did Steve Schrader ask you to change?*
A: The voice. The third-person narration seemed very distant, but the dialogue between the characters was a lot more lively. So what I did was, I rewrote the narrative in a more conversational, more idiomatic voice. I think that provided an interesting juxtaposition, a kind of call-and-reponse between the narrative voice and the characters.

Q: *Your voice and your use of language are unique in the way they recreate the rhythms of African American speech. Did anybody gave you a hard time about that?*
A: I think readers or editors either respond to that way of playing with language, or they don't. If you have a third-person narrative voice that seems to be talking as opposed to being written, some readers might assume that it's not serious, because it doesn't come with the gravitas of a third-person narrator in the Jamesian sense. A narrator with that sense of play or mischievousness may not be taken as seriously as a narrative voice whose expression is more formal.

Q: *How did the African American community respond to the book?*
A: Well, *Darktown Strutters* has had a very broad readership. I'm not altogether comfortable with the category of "the African American community," because I don't believe communities have uniform responses to anything. I think the book has had a significant black readership, but there was some uneasiness about the ways in which both whites and blacks used this grotesque form of representation of black people. The history is very unsettling, and there are a lot of people who don't necessarily want to engage in a story that creates that sort of discomfort.

Q: When you make people uncomfortable, you open yourself to a lot of criticism.
A: No question about it. But this goes to where the real stakes are. Writers shouldn't confirm our convenient assumptions about the way the world is. For me as a writer, I want to go to the places that *aren't* comforting, to address issues people *don't* necessarily want to talk about or acknowledge. If art has any purpose, it is to go into those areas where most of us fear to tread.

Q: One scene in Darktown Strutters *stands out in my mind: Jim, the former slave and minstrel show dancer, is invited by his girlfriend to escape to the North. He refuses, saying that the only way he can be free is to be on stage.*
A: That's a very unsettling moment in the book. Jim's sense of what she's offering him—freedom—is an abstraction, something that he doesn't know. In the 1840s or 1850s, escaping was a dangerous undertaking.

In many ways Jim already has taken flight, in his imagination, when he expresses himself by dancing. He has already experienced a very visceral sense of freedom through dance. He doesn't want to give that up for something that is a lot more chancy.

And then, this is a situation where readers can make their own judgments. I wasn't interested in judging Jim; I was interested in the precariousness of his situation and leaving it to readers to decide what they thought of his actions.

Q: For Jim, being a performer was both his slavery and his freedom.
A: It was what he was consigned to, and yet it became a source of freedom.

Q: Which is true of all artists. We're sort of consigned to this role.
A: Yes.

Q: Writers are often afraid of rejection because it makes us feel bad.

But in Jim's case, if people didn't like his performance, they would literally kill him.
A: Jim had to tread a very fine line. If people didn't appreciate his performance, he would be in serious physical danger. And of course it didn't help his situation that he refused to use black cork on his face.

Q: Does Jim's risk-taking reflect how you feel about yourself as an artist?
A: Absolutely. And the writers that I have the greatest regard for are precisely those who take risks. That's the standard that was set by writers who have been models for me. They gave me permission to take risks myself, to explore human behavior in all of its terror as well as its triumph, and to claim membership in this group of people who invent stories.

That's part of what the *use* of it is, is to take those risks.. But you have to accept the possibility that you could go into a free fall and break your neck. With each book or play that I've written, I've felt that the element of risk was always there. I'm always searching for the place where the stakes are highest, and where there's the greatest possibility of failure.

Q: Seven Stories Press gave you an advance for your latest novel, Push Comes to Shove, *but later decided not to publish it. How did you feel about that?*
A: I wasn't surprised, because this happened over a period of two years which involved at least two revisions. The first time the publisher read the book, my intuition was that I had not written the book that he thought I was going to write.

Q: Isn't it amazing, how you can sometimes sense it before the editor does? You get this sort of sinking feeling in your gut.
A: I did. Two years down the road, that editor acknowledged that he hadn't connected to the book at the earliest stage of the writing.

That's an issue of vision. I make a distinction between someone who's making a criticism of something that doesn't live up to the best of my intentions, and someone who is leveling criticism against my work because they don't think they're not enthusiastic about the story I've chosen to tell.

Q: *How do advise your students about dealing with rejection?*
A: I tell students that rejection is something they must go through. Ted Solotaroff said something that has stayed with me for the past twenty-five years. He said that the writers who sustain themselves as writers are not necessarily the most gifted or the most talented; they are those writers who can best deal with rejection. Because it's coming!

Rejection is an integral part of any creative endeavor. Not that you accept the judgment, but you accept its presence in whatever you're engaged in. It's not something that you should spend a lot of time taking personally. You shouldn't ask yourself the perennial question, 'Why me?' Well, why not? Because we all get our turn!

Q: *It must have done a lot for your self-confidence to have so many famous writers supporting you early in your career.*
A: No question about it! Being part of a community of writers who were both peers and mentors was indispensable. You need that as a bulwark against all the opinions and assumptions in the world, where your efforts are not necessarily going to be sanctioned. No one *asked* us to do any of this!

Q: *In fact, some people even asked us* not *to.*
A: Right! No group or individual compels us to answer the call of the muse. And so, if we answer the call, that's *our* responsibility. To expect that our decision to write is going to be validated in the world at large can be quite a disappointment.

I'm not saying that one doesn't hope that validation is forthcoming. I think that if you write long enough, with honesty and integrity, that your validation is in the work itself, and it will accrue over time.

For many writers, validation from the world at large is something that they don't experience in their lifetimes. But again, if that's enough to make you stop writing, then you shouldn't have begun in the first place!

Q: *Like the narrator of* Tragic Magic, *you refused induction into the armed services and served time in jail. How did that experience affect you?*
A: During the sixties, my contact with the extraordinary people I met in the Civil Rights Movement altered my feelings about my duty to my country. I experienced the pieties and time-honored expressions of the promise of America as falling far short of the mark. I wanted to lend my efforts to bringing that promise into being, not waiting for it to happen.

There's always going to be resistance when you take issue with the way things are done. If you're called to serve your country in a specific way and if you don't do that, it's perceived as a kind of betrayal. But for me there was no alternative but to cast my lot with the people who were taking issue with the status quo. That had everything to do with my decision to refuse to serve in the armed forces. For me, there was no other choice. That sense of rejection, of being on the outside, was the very place I wanted to be. I didn't *want* to be in the mainstream of what was considered acceptable.

Q: *Still, it must have been hard.*
A: It wasn't a walk in the park. But sometimes something that may be good *for* you may not necessarily be good *to* you. And it seems a bit odd to expect to be honored, or championed or congratulated if you do something that is against what is considered to be the norm. That raises questions as to whether you talked yourself into something that you haven't really internalized.

Trying to make a change for the better does not come with universal acceptance or praise. If you're looking for praise, then you're in the wrong business.

Q: *What would you consider to be your biggest artistic failure?*
A: Everything I've written ultimately involves failure, in terms of not expressing to the fullest what I had hoped. I think that happens in any creative project. I also think that the sense of not going as far as you would have liked, of your reach exceeding your grasp, is not necessarily a bad thing.

I see anything that involves failure as an attempt to take opportunities I missed in a prior work and to sustain that level of ambition in a new project. The work may be completely different in terms of subject matter, but what persists is the level of ambition, risk-taking, and acknowledging the failure that's part of the process.

When he won the National Book Award for *Invisible Man*, Ralph Ellison said he felt the novel had failed in eloquence. Now, this is one of the great novels of Twentieth Century! But he acknowledged that one element, in his own assessment, was a failure. And I think that is perhaps a testament to its greatness.

Someone once said to me that a novel is an extended piece of writing with something wrong with it. The something that is *wrong* with it, I think, can be as much a virtue as what is *right* with it. Because we are all flawed, and we are all works-in-progress as human beings. We spend our lives trying in some way to fulfill what has been called the better angels of our nature. But we never fly unimpeded. We never get our permanent set of wings.

FREDERICK BUSCH

"I have never taken rejection as an
obstacle to my writing. It has remained,
at times, an obstacle to my publishing."

*Even a well-established career can veer toward derailment through
sheer bad luck. On the very day Frederick Busch's collection* The
Children in the Woods *was released, the book's editor was fired
and the publishing house was shut down. Because the orphaned
book registered low sales, no one wanted to even look at his next
novel,* Girls.

But Busch persisted. The book finally found a publisher and
Girls *was named a* New York Times *Notable Book. Since then,
Busch has published other acclaimed novels,* A Memory of War
and The Night Inspector, *as well as essay collections including*
Letters to a Fiction Writer *and* A Dangerous Profession. *He has
been honored by a Guggenheim Fellowship and a PEN/Malamud
Award.*

*Busch was born in Brooklyn in 1941. Until his recent retire-
ment, he was Fairchild Professor of Literature at Colgate University
He lives in upstate New York.*

Q: *In the past twenty-plus years, you've published twenty-five books. What role has rejection played in your career?*
A: My career started with rejection, as most people's do. I was the opposite of an overnight success. I was full of effort and disappointment, and I wrote for years before I was published.

I spent many years writing at ten and twelve o'clock at night after a day's work—at a public relations syndicate in New York City, or at a school administration magazine in Greenwich, Connecticut, or during my early days of teaching at Colgate University. I wrote at night and I labored at my jobs during the day, and I had no luck with three novels and countless bad short stories.

I got some stories published by 1966, and I finally got a novel published in 1971. It was my fourth novel. I had been at it since 1962.

Q: *Why do you think it took you so long to get published?*
A: I was a slow learner! I never took creative writing courses. I just made all the mistakes it was possible to make.

Q: *And then you finally ran out of mistakes?*
A: No, I still have plenty of those. One continues to have many opportunities to find failure, and I am acquitting myself the same as I ever did. I'm a slow learner and I just keep working at it.

Q: *Among your early rejections, do any stand out in your mind?*
A: I tell this story in the introduction to a book I edited called *Letters to a Fiction Writer*. A writer who had come through Colgate told me to write to his agent. He said, "Write a hell of a good letter. Represent yourself well."

So I did, and I had a very charming response from this agent, inviting me to send him my novel. It took forever to get a response. I still remember greeting the mailman, and walking up to our rented house with his letter.

It began, "Dear Mr. Busch, What a pity that you can't write fiction as well as you write letters of inquiry." My introduction to *Letters to a Fiction Writer* is my nine-page reply to that agent, thirty years later.

Q: In fact, you wrote the whole book to serve as an antidote to that kind of hurtful letter. It seems to me that you have a very mature attitude toward rejection. Has that always been the case?
A: It is *not* the case now and it has never been the case. It's just that—isn't there a theatrical saying, "Never let them see you sweat?" Well, my motto has always been, "Never let them see you bleed." Simply because it's boring. One becomes a real bore going around complaining about how tough it is to get published, or to stay published, or to sell a million books.

It's a tough profession in a pretty cruelly unliterary world, and you get plenty of hard knocks, but there's nothing to be gained from going around whining. You owe it to the people you live with and the people who look to you for direction to survive it.

Q: How did you go about trying to get your first novels published?
A: The world of publishing was a good deal more literary then than it is now. There were lots of small publishing houses and editors who were willing to read unsolicited manuscripts. I could send them my books and they would read them, and they would pull for me to be good enough to be published. Apparently I never was, quite, until later.

Q: How did you finally get published for the first time?
A: I corresponded with a poet and novelist in Scotland named Robert Nye. I sent him a manuscript and I said, "What do you think of this?" I was at the point where I was really desperately looking to get better.

Instead of sending me a critique, he sent the book to his editor in England with his recommendation that she publish it. I got a telegram from Calder and Boyers, an avant-garde literary house in London that had published Samuel Beckett and Henry Miller. The telegram said, "Calder and Boyers offers two hundred pounds for world rights." In those days that was four hundred and eight dollars. And I thought my life had absolutely changed.

Q: Had it?
A: Well, I was a published author. And my wife, Judy, and I and our little baby, Ben, went to England. My publisher threw a party for me, and it felt very literary and life-changing. My life stayed the same, I think, but it felt quite wonderful at the time.

Q: What about your perception of yourself as a writer? Did that change?
A: Well, I finally felt that I *was* a writer. I had published two stories and now this little novel. A dreadful little book, I think. I'm afraid to reread it.

Q: What about the books that didn't get published? Were they any good?
A: I don't think they were good. I didn't know how to write a novel yet. I was filled with language, and it was sometimes very good, very interesting, and very musical language, but I didn't know how to tell a story yet.

My first novel was very badly received by publishers to whom I sent it. After it was rejected, I got myself into a state of desperation and blankness. I knew I had to go on and learn to write a novel, and I knew that, to do that, I had to write a second manuscript. I had a lot of energy, which is a resource a good writer needs. But I couldn't get started.

Around that time, I read a poem by Galway Kinnell called "The Bear," which is as much about poetry as it as about the natural world. It's a great poem, and it blasted me loose. It moved me out of my paralysis.

Q: What was it about Kinnell's poem that got you so fired up?
A: His total dedication to the world of the poem. That poem sang itself to me about writing and the great animal vitality of the writer, and it brought me inside its magic boundaries.

I still remember the thrill with which I sat down at a legal pad with a fountain pen and began to write a second novel based on the rhythms and the music of "The Bear." I had that joy in spite of being unpublished, unheralded, and unthanked. That thrill of taking up Galway Kinnell's music, and being caused by it to make music of my own on the page, is still palpable to me.

I was writing for the love of the writing as much as to be published, and I have been supported by that, girded by that, driven by that all my adult working life. I still feel that kind of thrill when I write.

Q: It seems to me that if you don't have that, it's impossible to go on.
A: Unless you're a cold, calculating writer of bodice-rippers—you know, genre books—and you're doing it because it's your job. Some people can do that, bless them! I don't decry it. But I'm trying to make something beautiful and I have always loved the attempt.

Q: Still, those first few years must have been frustrating!
A: What made it worse was, I had read someplace that John Updike and Philip Roth had each published his first book before his twenty-seventh birthday. Naturally I set that impossible goal for myself. And when I hit twenty-seven and was as unpublished as ever, I found it crushing.

I think I was thirty-one before my first novel was published. And it surely didn't make the splash that Updike's or Roth's books did. It wasn't nearly as good as either of theirs was, so it didn't *deserve* to make a splash.

But I kept comparing myself to larger figures and setting these impossible goals. If I could advise myself as I was then, I would say, "Take it easy, kid! Just do your job, and when it's time, you *will* be published." If we could all tell ourselves that, we would have a lot less pain. But one of the factors in our lives, if we have literary talent, is ambition, and it goads us. That's what makes us not give up, but it also is what makes us so unhappy with ourselves.

Q: Why do we writers need to be published so badly?
A: For me, I want to tell a story, which is a transitive transaction. I want to tell the story *to* someone, and to do that, you need to be published.

There have been times in my career when, because of a confluence of bad luck, bad events, bad management. I have felt that I was in danger of being extinguished as a writer. But I would never stop writing.

I remember at one particular point, I thought I was going to have to get used to never being published again. It was pretty well into my career, in the early 1990s. What had happened was that, on the day that a book of my new and selected stories was published, not only was my editor fired, but the publishing house was shut down.

Q: Oh, no!
A: Here was this big, fat book of stories called *The Children in the Woods: New and Selected Stories*, which I love. It's beautifully produced, but without anybody behind it, it was totally orphaned. There was nobody to sell it, and it did terribly.

As a result, instead of being associated with the novel before it, which had sold well, I seemed to be known for *The Children in the Woods*. When it came to my next novel, *Girls*, people turned it down left and right because of the numbers clocked into the computer.

It didn't seem right to me and it didn't seem fair, but these things never are fair. There is no fairness in sales, and that's all that publishers care about—with a very few wonderful exceptions.

So I was pretty close to saying, "Well, I'll keep writing, but I'll keep writing for me." But fortunately I have a brilliant agent. She managed to do what I think of as bypass surgery. She got around those numbers and got some editors to care about the book.

Girls went on to be a very good seller, and it was appreciated critically. I've been somewhat safe since then, but one is almost always available to bad luck unless you're a proven cash cow for the publishers.

Q: When you decided to keep on writing, what was your thought process?
A: That *was* the thought process. I thought, "I can't stop writing because I love to do it. I love to tell stories and I love to make language, and my life is predicated on doing that. I'm not going to end my life for those bastards, so I'll keep writing." It was a pretty simple thought process. There seemed to be no room for argument.

Q: When you taught writing at Colgate University, did you advise students about these issues?
A: I didn't permit my undergraduate students to deal with these issues! I always made them keep their eye on learning how to write, not learning how to publish.

When I dealt with graduate students and encountered their lust to publish—and you can't blame them—I was always happy to give them practical advice. But when I was teaching undergraduates, my advice tended to be mostly about the form of the story.

Q: In other words, you feel that students shouldn't try to publish when they're not ready?
A: I don't think *anybody* should try to publish when he's not ready! That goes for seventy-five-year-olds who have been writing for thirty-five years. If it's not time, master your craft!

People have said to me, "Just once before I die, I want to be published." I obviously understand those words, because they're in my native tongue. But I've never understood wanting to be published before you know how to write something *worthy* of being published. Sometimes I have to say, "Look, I don't think it's time."

Q: Looking back, was it "not time" for your first three novels?
A: At the time I *thought* it was time. I yearned with all my heart to have those books published. But I'm pretty sure now that I'm lucky they weren't.

Q: Herman Melville is a main character in your novel, The Night Inspector. *Did you learn anything about rejection from his career?*
A: What we all learn from Melville is how not to mismanage your career. He had a wretched, absolutely ghastly career. He couldn't help it, I guess—he was driven by debt, as well as by a hunger to be an author and tell his stories. I mean, he ended up writing *Billy Budd* at night after a day working at the customs house, when he knew that no one would publish him again. What astonishing courage and dedication to craft!

Each book after that was received less well. After *Moby Dick* came *Pierre.* After those books came *Israel Potter,* and nobody wanted to know. He had no support from his publishers, and ultimately even the reviewers who had liked him turned against him. He said it himself: "What I will write, won't sell. What I must write, I don't wish to write."

Q: "I would prefer not to."
A: Yes! If Melville had wanted to succeed, he would have had to write semi-salacious, quasi-factual combinations of memoir and plagiarism like *Typee,* his first book, which was very successful. But he wanted less and less to do that. He wanted to follow his vision, and he really had no choice.

Q: What could he possibly have done differently?
A: Well, some people write only to sell. He certainly couldn't do

that. And some people suppress what would become literature in order to have a career, and he certainly would not do that. He's the great horror figure for us all.

Q: *Did he die a bitter and unhappy person?*
A: I suspect he did. I think there was probably too much drinking and despair and anger. He became more and more inward, and more and more difficult to penetrate as a writer.

Q: *When you look back on Melville's career, do you admire him for following his vision?*
A: You have to. You have to be frightened for yourself, because none of us has his brains and talent, and if he can fail, we can fail. He was a brave man. He was a brave, difficult, cranky, impenetrable man.

Q: *You also wrote a novel,* The Mutual Friend, *in which Charles Dickens is the main character. Did you learn anything from his career?*
A: I have learned an awful lot about writing and language from Dickens. It's harder to apply his career to that of someone as small as I am. He was the most important writer of his time in the whole world, and I don't have talent like that.

I think Dickens had the most resolute of ambitions, the greatest will, the hugest determination to be independent and to chart his own course. He was a great businessman as well as a writer, and he used his resources brilliantly. I'm just not in his league. So I didn't learn anything about managing a career from him, except what I can envy.

Q: *Did he have to face many rejections before he got published?*
A: No. He started out successful. Even though some books did less well than others, he was a hugely venerated and successful author.

There were plenty of people to knock him and to criticize him. But Dickens could do what only a handful of contemporary authors can do: write what they want, and reach the public directly.

Q: *He was like Stephen King.*
A: Exactly. That's the name that comes to mind. No matter how many bad reviews King gets—and he usually deserves them—it doesn't matter. People reach for his books automatically, just as he reaches out to them. There are a few other writers like that, but King is the best example.

Q: *It's interesting that you have chosen to write about Melville and Dickens, who are at opposite extremes in terms of how they were received by the public.*
A: But that's not why I chose them. I was simply drawn to their genius. And God knows what kind of hubris made me think I could write a novel with Melville in it. I was in terror every morning as I went in to write. It was like writing a casual short story about God. It was a fearful undertaking, accompanied by all kinds of trepidations.

Q: *Speaking of trepidation, tell me how you deal with criticism.*
A: I try not to read my reviews. I'd just as soon not know. Because if you respect what they say about you that's good, then somehow, through some cosmic sense of justice, you have to respect what they say about you that's bad. And I don't want to.

The reviewing game is a radically imperfect system. It tends to require a one-time, hasty reading of an imperfect text—that is, a set of proofs with mistakes in them. You've got a second-rate text being read by someone who can only read the book once and who's got a deadline. And that's to assume that the reviewer is smart, experienced with literature, and understanding of the demands of the form that you're attempting.

I don't like something I've worked on for a couple of years, and to which I have given numerous pints of my blood, to be judged on the run by somebody who doesn't understand the venture. But you have to smile and be a good sport and not let them see you bleed, as I said before.

Most fiction writers I know are fiction writers to the bone and in the bone. They just have to do it, whether the book sells well this time out or it doesn't, whether the great panjandrum in some newspaper loves them or doesn't. It's not irrelevant, but in a way it is, because the main thing is the writing.

Q: *What kind of advice do you give to writers who are discouraged about getting published?*
A: Well, you know, you can only bolster them so much. If they get discouraged, then maybe that's good. If they get out of the game, it's a kind of Darwinian elimination of a creature whose genes you don't want in the pool.

If you want to be published, nail your feet to the floor and do the work. Of course it's discouraging. But look at it this way: You're asking publishers to spend money on your work, and to risk being fired for having published people like you. They're going to lose their jobs; their families are going to starve! You've got no right to whine.

Q: *You once gave this advice: "Never use 'submit' as a word for sending work to magazine or book publishers." What did you mean by that?*
A: Even though we probably *are* submissive, we shouldn't put ourselves in the position of *feeling* submissive. "Dear Sir, I hope you like this," is what we say. But we could equally say, with a little dignity, "Dear Sir, I think this would be a good book for you to publish. Here is something by me that you may, if you mind your manners, have."

I don't think that either of our agents sends our work out with a note that says, "Here's Cathy Wald's newest, I hope you don't hate it. I wonder if you would do us all a favor and publish it." That's what 'submit' suggests.

I mean, let's be a little proud of ourselves. "Here is a good book that I wrote, I want you to publish it, please." Whether or not you *say* that, that should be the attitude. It's just a little mental health vitamin pill.

Q: It sounds to me as if you have never taken rejection as a great obstacle.
A: I have never taken it as an obstacle to my doing more writing. It has remained, at times, an obstacle to my publishing.

Q: Besides rejection, what are some of your biggest challenges as a writer?
A: Demanding of myself that I show up for work every day and write the best I can; not giving in to sorrow or eagerness or haste or fear; not being afraid of the subject matter or the linguistic effort or the structure I'm trying to arrive at; and writing the book I want to write—not the book I think a book club or a movie director will want.

Q: You write what you will *write, not what you* must *write. At least in that way, you're just like Melville, after all!*
A: Yes, I guess I am.

DAVID EBERSHOFF

JACOB LLOYD

"Rejection will happen throughout your career
at different levels. You have to be fearless about it."

*As a novelist and publishing director of the Modern Library
imprint at Random House, David Ebershoff has a unique perspective on publication and rejection. Born in 1969 in Pasadena, he
published his first novel when he was in his early thirties.* The
Danish Girl *was called "heartbreaking and unforgettable" by the*
Boston Globe *and was selected as a* New York Times *Notable
Book. Since then, he has published the novel* Pasadena *and a short
story collection* The Rose City. *He lives in New York City and has
taught fiction writing at New York and Princeton universities.*

Q: *Before we go into your background as an editor, let's talk about
your history as a writer.*
A: I began writing short stories when I was fifteen. By the time I
was twenty-one, I thought I should start sending them to literary magazines. I started going through the very slow process of
putting them in the mail and waiting for months to get them

back with a little slip of paper that's only a little bigger than the piece of paper in a fortune cookie.

At the time, I kept an 8½ by 11" notebook. I would tape the rejections in as reminders of what I'd done. They were badges of courage.

Q: I guess putting them in a notebook is a little more discreet than pasting them on your walls, like some writers do.
A: Theoretically nobody has, or ever will, read this notebook. And only after at least one hundred of these rejections, did I get one with a handwritten note on it. In addition to the little phrase that was typed up on the note saying, "We appreciate you sending this in, but we can't use it and wish you luck," somebody had written "Sorry." It was a rejection, but it was different enough from the previous hundred rejections for me to feel that I could continue to make a go of this.

Q: Why didn't that handwritten "sorry" make you depressed or angry?
A: Well, this came, in context, after a hundred blanks—just scraps of paper with the story coming back in the mail. I had no sense of, Was it read? What happened to it? After many, many dozens of rejections, to get one coming in with a hand-written note—I felt like there was at least a little time spent with my story.

I felt that a little personalization was a slight sign that the story meant something more than most of the slush pile. That was my hunch, and I do think it's pretty accurate, because I eventually became a fiction editor at *Chicago Review*. The mail was just a torrent; we had nine hundred submissions a month. We would read them, and most of the time we would just return them with a Xerox, because there was no time and because most of the stories were *so* not right for us.

Sometimes a story doesn't work, but you know talent. You know a half-good story, and there were so few of them that you got excited about them. Any time we felt like there was a sign of talent, or a story that interested us enough to think about it, we *did* personalize.

Q: *Maybe writers who get upset about notes like that don't understand how overwhelmed editors are.*
A: Yes. I also think that if you're a writer, it gets back to this question: Can you let something like that stop you? And if something like that stops you, *are* you a writer? Rejection will happen. It's going to happen throughout your career at different levels. You have to be fearless about it.

And it does depend on where you are in your work. If you're writing something and it's going really well you can still feel really confident as a writer when a rejection comes through. Whereas if you *haven't* been writing, and you have all your hopes in the piece on submission, then the rejection hurts more.

That's why I think the best advice people can get before their first book is published is: Get yourself into your next book. That is going to help you keep everything in perspective, and it's going to be your ballast. If things don't go well, you're still going to have your core—which is your next book. And if everything goes well, and you may become a crazy, successful phenomenon, you're still going to need your core—which is your next book.

Q: *How many times were you rejected before you had anything accepted?*
A: Maybe one hundred and fifty times. I didn't feel as if the magazines were necessarily wrong in rejecting my stories, but I also didn't doubt myself as a writer. I somehow knew that that was part of the process.

I think, ultimately, every writer feels as if he has no choice. We're going to continue to write into rejection because we're writers. This is what we do; in fact it's what we *want* to do. It's what we enjoy spending our time on more than anything.

Q: Tell me about the influence of Harriet Doerr on your career as a writer.

A: I'm from suburban Southern California, so fiction writers seemed like a foreign breed. And then, all of a sudden, when I was eleven or twelve, there was Harriet Doerr living next door. Harriet Doerr graduated from Stanford University in her late sixties and stayed on as a Stegner Fellow. She published her first novel, *Stones for Ibarra,* when she was seventy-two—and it won the National Book Award.

For a long time, Harriet Doerr was the only writer I knew. While I was growing up and beginning to think that I wanted to be a writer, that was my measurement. I thought I would keep trying until I was seventy-two, and then maybe I would have to give up at that point.

Q: Did you always know you wanted to get involved in the publishing industry?

A: No. Being from the West Coast, the East Coast world of publishing and writers seemed very clubby, and certainly something I couldn't be a part of. When I was in my senior year at Brown University, I was walking by the Career Services Office, and I saw a poster saying, "Random House will be on campus interviewing seniors." I looked at it and I thought, "Oh, my God, Random House! Wouldn't that be a wonderful place to work? But I could never get a job there." And I just walked on.

Q: You self-rejected.

A: I self-rejected, and it wasn't until years later that I tried. I have done that in many things in my life. But the one thing that I have always pushed myself hardest on, in terms of sailing through rejection, is my writing—because to me, it's not a choice.

There was a point after college when I applied to writing programs. I was twenty-three or twenty-four and I was beginning to feel a little confident about my fiction. I applied to all the writing programs you could imagine, and I was rejected by all of them. But I think it was a very fortunate rejection.

Q: Why?
A: Looking back on it now, I don't think they made a mistake. I don't think I was there yet as a writer.

That rejection was the most significant rejection in my writing career. As surprised and embarrassed as I was by it, I wasn't going to let it stop me. I just said, "Well, the only thing I can do about this is write."

Q: It sounds like you grew up with a very solid sense of what you wanted to do.
A: I did. But I didn't talk about it much. I was not prepared to share the rejection. I could bear it on my own, but I couldn't bear everyone *knowing* that I was being rejected. That was my method of self-protection from the profound embarrassment I thought I would have if people knew I was sending out stories that nobody wanted to publish and, by implication, that nobody would want to read.

Q: With all your experience as an editor and a teacher, can you tell pretty quickly from someone's work whether they were meant to be a writer or not?
A: If I know anything about editing and teaching, it's this: You can know if something fundamentally doesn't work, but no one can tell anyone who should or should not be a writer. You just can't know that based on reading something.

Often my strongest reaction to my students' work is that they have some level of talent, but they haven't found what they should be writing about. I often think, "Oh, this writer just needs to find her material—the story that truly is going to engage her."

Q: Do you give your students advice about how to handle rejection?
A: No, but I *do* talk about revision. Revision is, in part, a

response to internal rejection. You read your own work and say, "This isn't working." That kind of self-rejection is key to nearly all writers.

Q: You wrote a novel that you said was really bad. At the time, did you know it wasn't marketable?
A: I didn't know anything. I was in college, and I sent it directly to publishing houses, not knowing that that was a very unwise thing to do. It came back months and months later with a Xeroxed note from the publishing houses. But what I got out of it was this notion that I'd managed to write a story, carry it through, conclude it, and revise it—and maybe I would manage to do it again.

Q: Are you glad now that it wasn't published?
A: Absolutely! It shouldn't have been; it couldn't have been; it never *would* have been.

Q: How did The Danish Girl *get published?*
A: When I had been working on it for eight or nine months, I thought, "Maybe I should think about getting an agent." In the back of my mind remembering all these rejections and thinking, "I can go through the process, but nothing will happen." And also being OK with that, because I was so far from being seventy-two years old.

At this point I was still in sales and marketing at Random House, and I had no contacts with agents. I sent out query letters and I was flat-out rejected by three or four agents. But one wrote me a very professional editorial memo, with astute insights into some of the problems and issues in the book. It was a useful letter written with great compassion to the writer—a very generous gesture for an agent to make.

Q: You never told anyone at work that you wrote fiction. Why?
A: Again, I couldn't face a public rejection. Random House is a

heady place to work. You're very aware of who has been published here, and who is being published here, and I couldn't bring myself to say, "I want to be a part of that." I didn't want that scrutiny.

There's a great bliss to writing peacefully on your own, when nobody knows anything about what you're doing, when your own ideas can be shaped and molded, and no expectations have been set for it. That's especially true in the beginning of a novel. It's such a quiet time—just you and the idea and the characters.

Q: *Once you found an agent,* The Danish Girl *sold quickly.*
A: It was at a pace that I'd never imagined possible, and I was astonished and entirely grateful. But, you know, one of the ways I dealt with that moment was one of the ways I continue to deal with the ups and downs of being a published writer, which is: "It happened, but I still have a job to go to, where I work for other writers."

My effort has to be on my writing my books, and working on the books Random House publishes. The other stuff I can't give too much time to—whether it's rejection or acceptance, actually. I'm the type of person who doesn't get as much pleasure out of reading a good review as I get devastation from reading a bad review. It doesn't do enough for me as a writer to spend all that time parsing somebody else's words. And I would be wasting time that I could use either publishing a book or writing a book.

When I'm writing a book, that's what I care about. I'm pinning all my hopes to it and to the keyboard—not to the reviews that are running today or last month. There are only so many things I focus on, and I try to remember what's important.

Q: *Don't you celebrate even a little bit when you get good reviews?*
A: When my first book came out, I got a lovely fax from Joyce Carol Oates. She said, "Congratulations on the reviews for *The Danish Girl.* Not that reviews are 'real,' but when they're celebratory, we should rejoice."

That meant a lot to me. Praise, obviously is nice and we should be grateful, but that's not the task. The task is about sitting at the desk and getting to work and solving the problems of the story. That's all that matters, and that's when we're happiest.

Certainly the good things are good, and you have to be grateful for them and acknowledge them. But that's not going to help you the next morning at the computer—except in the realm of confidence, maybe.

If you were praised in the newspaper one day, maybe the next day you'll go to your work with the right amount of confidence. Then again, you can always have too much confidence. And if you got a bad review, you may doubt yourself. That is why I can't get into that. I have enough self-doubt while I'm working out the story. I don't need other people to contribute to it.

Q: As an editor, what have you learned about why writers are rejected?
A: Some rejections have complications that the writer will never know about. A house can turn something down because they have something similar in the works, or because there's a question about the size of the market. Sometimes there's a feeling that it's a fine book, and it'll be published, but it may not be right for this house. Other times a manuscript can end up with the wrong editor. And all that will not get back to the author. It's just going to feel like a rejection.

Q: Have you ever been rejected as an editor?
A: Sometimes books can be rejected in the reviews, or they don't sell, and you do feel rejected as an editor. You can't sit in the park all day with a cigarette moaning about it, but it doesn't make you feel good.

If the reviews are good and the book doesn't take off, you at least have *that* to feel good about. It's no consolation in terms of the financial obligation. But as an editor, you always have some books that are working and some that aren't working. Whereas if you're an author and your book isn't working, that's the end of the story.

Q: Do you believe that if a book is really of a high caliber, it will eventually get published?
A: I do believe that a truly good book is going to find its way into the world. You could think of it this way. A very good writer's first book may not make it. But that very good writer is then going to go and write another very good book, which eventually is going to make it. Then the world will want to know about what came before.

BRET EASTON ELLIS

MARION ETTLINGER

"If I had believed what everyone had written
about *American Psycho*, I don't know
if I would have ever written another book."

When his first book, Less Than Zero, *was published, twenty-one-
year-old Bret Easton Ellis was hailed as the voice of a new generation. His fiction has sparked controversy ever since, especially*
American Psycho, *the grisly, graphically detailed story of a rich,
young and handsome serial killer. Just a week before publication,
portions of the book were leaked to the press, generating a feminist uproar and even death threats, and publisher Simon and
Schuster dropped it.*

*When Vintage published the novel, the ranting continued. "A
contemptible piece of pornography," "deeply and extremely disgust-
ing," "devoid of morals" were a few of the critical reactions. So were
"brilliant," "hilarious," and "important."*

Amazingly, Ellis never let the firestorm of controversy around
American Psycho *make him doubt himself as a writer. Since then,
he's published* The Informers *and* Glamorama, *as well as many
articles in* Rolling Stone, Vanity Fair, Vogue, *and* Interview. *His*

books American Psycho, Less Than Zero, *and* Rules of Attraction *have been made into feature films.*

Q: Your first book, Less Than Zero, *was published when you were still a student at Bennington College. It had much more success than you'd anticipated.*
A: This is true. It came totally out of the blue.

Q: Was it as a mixed blessing?
A: When I look at being published that early, part of me thinks, "Wow, that was great! To jump over all those hurdles so effortlessly, to not have to deal with how tough the publishing business can be, to be able to meet so many older writers who you admired, and to have all the doors open so effortlessly—all that was a good thing."

I didn't know anything about publishing when *Less Than Zero* came out. When it became a bestseller, I assumed that that just *happened* to books. I really didn't get that it was a big deal.

You know, it was a unique case. It was a unique time in publishing, it was a unique book, and the way people responded to it was, again, unique. I really don't see that happening much now. I do see first novels that get wildly praised and are big successes, but usually the writers aren't twenty-one, and usually the books aren't defined by the press as *the* book about a generation. It was a unique position to be in, and right now I can only look at it positively.

Q: But didn't you have a nervous breakdown after Less Than Zero *was published?*
A: Well, that was inevitable. Maybe it would have happened a year or two later, but my makeup was heading toward that no matter what. The success and the pressure of what had happened probably just speeded it up.

If I was depressed, and if there was anxiety in that initial period, I think a lot of it had to do with the fact that I was just twenty-one. At that age, you still don't know that much about life yet.

Q: Would you say that the first time you experienced professional rejection was when American Psycho *was published?*
A: My first book, *Less Than Zero,* was not regarded as a great book at the time it was published. The reviews were very mixed. In the *New York Times Book Review,* I think the reviewer actually wrote, "I hated reading this book." Again, I think that was good. Going through an experience where I was poorly reviewed part of the time toughened me up a little bit for the bad reviews I got in the future.

I think the first real whiff of professional rejection I got was with the publication of my second book, *The Rules of Attraction.* Though it sold very well, it definitely didn't do *Less Than Zero*-type business, and the reviews were very cruel and mean.

Q: How did you react to the criticism of The Rules of Attraction?
A: At the time I kind of did live up to the persona that the press had already painted me as—this decadent party boy—when, in fact, I wasn't any more decadent than most of the people in my generation. I was twenty-three. That's what twenty-three-year-olds do.

I guess the press resented the fact that I didn't take the whole publication process—I don't know what—more seriously? And I had become successful and I wasn't living in some hovel someplace and writing late at night with a quill pen. I mean, I think they expected me to take everything much more seriously than I did. And I suppose if I was older, I would have.

And then we go straight to the *real* rejection. The whole controversy surrounding *American Psycho,* was a much more obvious, much more intense, much more vast and overwhelming rejection.

Q: Many people were upset about the graphic violence in American Psycho, *where the protagonist, Patrick Bateman, spends a great deal of time torturing, mutilating, and murdering people for no particular reason. However, it was the outcry from feminist groups like the National Organization for Women that pressured the original publisher, Simon and Schuster, to pull the plug on the project. What do you remember most about the big brouhaha?*

A: I remember thinking, "All this is not based on anything that's real. I'll get through this because I believe in the book."

I watched with a curious detachment as this avalanche occurred in slow motion. I guess that's the best way I can describe it. I was in disbelief, because the criticism wasn't based on anything concrete, but once the ball started rolling, it was just unstoppable. People picked up on the story and they rolled with it without reading the book, or getting the book, or understanding how all these things had happened that turned it into a scandal. The ball got bigger, and then it got bigger, and then it just got out of control.

It *was* shocking. I have to say that. It was definitely a shocking thing, but in the end it didn't necessarily totally—let's put it that way—cause me to unravel.

Q: Define "totally."
A: Well, it was distracting enough that I didn't write for a little while. It was distracting enough that I did lose focus on the book I was working on at the time. But for some reason I knew, even after the *New York Times* ran a review with the title, "Snuff This Book," that ten years down the road this book would still be in print, and it would be selling more copies than ever.

Q: And you were right.
A: The reaction to that book now is totally the opposite of what the reaction was when it was first published.

Q: By the way, I thought the book was hilarious.
A: Well that's the other weird thing. People took the book so

insanely seriously, and they wrote about it so humorlessly. I always saw the book as a very funny book, as a black comedy.

Of course, you should have been gasping at times, too. I reread the book recently; and it was shocking. There's a lot of stuff in there that's pretty hard-core and that, as the guy of thirty-nine that I am today, I would not touch. But if you weren't laughing when you were reading that book, then you didn't get it.

That also made moving through that scandal easier. If I had believed what everyone had written about that book at the time of its publication, I don't know if I would have ever written another book.

Q: Why do you think you were able to keep your perspective?
A: Quite honestly, writing workshops. The writing workshops that I was in, in college, were pretty vicious. And people at Bennington were extremely serious. A lot of well-known writers came out of my class: Jonathan Lethem, Donna Tartt, Jill Eisenstadt.

Bennington had a very competitive, intense atmosphere. People definitely had their criticisms and negative reactions to stories you'd present. That's an important growing process for a writer, because you develop an armor against criticism. It isn't an armor against editing by people who understand your work and offer you constructive ideas on how to solve certain problems. But it really gave me a very hard shell. And the other thing is, I never *agreed* with any of it. And that carried over to when I was professionally published.

Q: You obviously got a lot out of the Bennington workshops besides just getting toughened up.
A: Oh, yeah! I recommend them wholeheartedly. I had really good teachers, and I wrote a lot of good stuff. But you have to take them realistically. You have to understand that a) If you're not a writer, they're not going to make you a writer, and b) If you can't take criticism, just don't bother going into them, and c) If

you're not able to read your classmates' work objectively and fairly, also don't.

Q: *The criticism of* American Psycho *didn't bother you very much was because it didn't ring true?*
A: Right. There have been certain reviews throughout my career that have stung, because the writer had really tussled with the book and obviously understood my intention, and completely disagreed. That actually happens very rarely. Those are the ones where you go, "Ouch, he's right about that."

But with *American Psycho,* I didn't feel that way at all. The reviews at the time were so hysterical. They were based on a moral position rather than an aesthetic one, so it was very easy to disregard them.

My work tends to be reviewed from a more moralistic viewpoint than any of my contemporaries. The aesthetic point is often buried in a lot of hand-wringing about the vacuity of my characters, the violence, etc. It's very rare for me to find someone grappling with the aesthetics of the work.

Being reviewed is not part of the creative process. You're working alone in your apartment for two, three, four years on a novel. And then nine months later it comes out, and there are all these people saying things about it that are either very confusing or have nothing to do with your intentions. Even if they love it, they love it for reasons that confuse you.

In the end, if you have to have reviews, let's face it, you want good ones. But even as I say that, there are certain reviewers that I don't really particularly *want* a good review from, knowing their track record. If they responded positively, I would feel that I had written the wrong kind of book.

You know what? You're only human. There are flashes of disappointment when close friends or family members don't get what you were doing. But then again, I'm going to give you the obvious cliché: You don't write for your mom, you don't write for your family, you don't write for anyone but yourself.

I had a very critical, very demanding father. I think that also toughens you up a lot. You learn that there are a lot worse things than a bad review; there are a lot worse things than someone not liking your story; and there are a lot worse things than someone not getting your book.

Q: You once said that you might never have become a writer without having had an abusive father. Do you still look at it that way?
A: Totally. That's one of the big paradoxes about my feelings about my father. There was a lot of rage, disappointment, and negative feelings. At the same time I do think that our relationship shaped me into who I became. Although in years of therapy, I have tried to change that to some degree.

My father definitely was part of the reason I became a writer. There was a part of me that felt buried under his anger. I felt mute, and writing was a way of expressing myself, even if just to myself.

Q: Have you ever written anything about your dad?
A: Patrick Bateman of *American Psycho* was, in part, based on my father's values and the way he lived his life. What he felt was important was status and surface appearances. All that tended to overwhelm his life, and I think it made him very frustrated and angry. He became a very empty, sad person because he believed that money meant everything, that it defined you and gave you freedom.

At the same time, there's a lot of Patrick Bateman is me as well. When I wrote that book I was very young, I was very angry, I was very depressed, and I was at my most nihilistic. It was the angry young man syndrome—an artist, coming of age, realizes that this is the way the world works, and writes something to denounce that.

Q: What do you consider your biggest obstacle in your writing life?
A: During the nineties, the biggest obstacles were distractions in

my life: the *American Psycho* controversy, my father's death, drugs and alcohol, the breakup of a seven-year relationship. I really do agree with Flaubert's dictum that in order to write like a revolutionary, you need to live like a bourgeois. I do think there needs to be a certain comfort level where there's not a lot of worry, a lot of dread, or a lot of bad things happening in your life. You need to be in a good place to work on a book, no matter what the subject matter is.

Q: Was the publication of American Psycho *a defining moment in your career?*
A: The things that are more important to me professionally are things that no one else noticed. For me, a professional high point was having Joan Didion dedicate a book (*After Henry*) to me. That tops whatever great reviews I've had or how many books I've sold.

When I look back on my career, often the things that were most exciting to me were certain days when I was working on a novel and something that I had planned unexpectedly merged into something even better than I could have hoped for. Those are the days that make all the other days—when you get a page done, maybe, and you're so depressed, and you think the book you're working on is a total piece of shit, and you don't have any faith in your writing talents—those are the days that make it all worthwhile. And they're very private moments.

When I finished *Glamorama* after eight years of work, I was alone in my apartment. It was totally quiet, and this huge journey that I'd been on ended kind of unexpectedly. That's something you really can't share with anyone else. There were no balloons coming down, no confetti, no one jumping up and down. I just sat there, a huge wave of relief washed over me, and I took a shower and got dressed and went to dinner.

JANET FITCH

CLAUDIA KUNIN

"You don't need to be published, you
don't need to be accepted, you don't need
anybody's seal of approval to write."

*"What's unique about your sentences?" That was the challenge
flung out by the rejection letter, and budding writer Janet
Fitch took it to heart. But first she had to figure out what it meant.*

Fitch, author of the bestselling novel White Oleander, *served a
long apprenticeship as a fiction writer. As she learned how to tell a
story, she had to brave a tough mentor, many rejection letters, and
isolation from other writers. Then, only a month after its publication,* White Oleander *was selected for Oprah's Book Club, and
Fitch had to learn a whole new lesson: how to deal with success.*

*A native of Los Angeles, Fitch has taught at UCLA's Writing
Program and California State University, Fullerton. In Fall 2001
she served as the first Mosely Fellow in Creative Writing at Pomona
College. She has also worked as a typesetter, a graphic artist, and a
freelance journalist.*

Q: In your experience, how important is rejection in a writer's career?

A: Rejection plays an overwhelming role in your career. When my students start sending out stories, I tell them, "Until you have a hundred rejections, you're really not a writer."

Q: How did you come up with the number one hundred?
A: Well, that gives them a sense of proportion. Because when you start writing, you think you're going to sell your first story. Then, when you get four rejections, or when your *second* story gets four rejections, you're just crushed.

One hundred rejections is just a start. You have to think of them as, "Oh, God, another one out of the way. I need to have these rejections, because they indicate that I'm getting my work out in the marketplace." It is crushing, and you work with the cumulative effect of all that rejection. But that's a lot of what being a writer is.

Rejection is not only about sending your work out; it's also showing your stuff to people with a good idea about writing. The ability to withstand critique is the first step in learning how to handle rejection. You get a more objective idea of the quality of what you are sending out, and then the rejection is easier to see as just one person's opinion. Whereas when you're not getting critiqued, the rejection seems to be, "God has spoken."

Q: Some writers find it harder to listen to critiques in a class than to handle rejections they get in the mail.
A: With critique you have to learn who to listen to and who not to listen to. You have to recognize what rings true, which often hurts the worst. When somebody sees it right on, it resonates in a way that unfair or inappropriate critique doesn't.

Q: Have you ever had a positive rejection?
A: Yes. A rejection that changed my life came from the *Santa Monica Review.* The story had been rejected by many people before that, but what Jim Krusoe, the editor, wrote was, "Good

enough story, but what's unique about your sentences?" And that rejection drove me *wild*!

Q: It would drive me wild.
A: What the hell did he mean? What the hell did he want me to do—put the adjectives at the end? What's unique about my sentences?

That was really a challenge for me to become a better writer and to upgrade my art. I had been getting rejected without knowing why. To get a bit of specific information from some-body who sees a lot of stories—that was a gift from the universe, even if it hurt. I just cherish that.

It took me ten years to sell my first short story. And you don't know why, and you don't know why, and you don't know why. And here was someone saying, "Here's why. You can tell a story, but you're not looking on the micro level. Pay attention to the sentences themselves."

Q: What did you do to address that criticism?
A: I started thinking about sentences. I went and got an old-fash-ioned grammar and started trying to diagram sentences. I looked at the sentences of really fine stylists, people I really admire, and I started trying to figure out how they were put together.

I sought out Kate Braverman's workshop because of that sen-tence thing. I was looking for someone to help me into the art of the sentence; so I got somebody who had a background as a poet. Working with her made the difference between being a good storyteller and really learning the art. It was my first expe-rience with a really fine teacher and a tremendously talented group of writers. The level of critique was *so* high, and the stan-dards were *so* high. That's when I started working hardest.

Q: And yet, that workshop was a difficult experience.
A: Let's just put it this way. I was once a fan of Carlos Castaneda's books. At one point, there are these two sorcerers—

don Juan, who is Castaneda's teacher, and another teacher named don Genaro. Castaneda points out to don Juan that don Genaro's students have fun, and they're always laughing. He asks, "Why aren't you like that?" And don Juan says, "There's the hard teacher and the soft teacher, and you just happened to get the hard teacher." And that's what I got.

I teach, too, and I find that your teaching style is a reflection of your personality. It doesn't really have much to do with the quality of the instruction. If a student wants what someone is teaching, they're going to stand up to it because they *need* what's being taught so badly.

I would have put up with anything, because what I was getting was so valuable. And ultimately that's the dividing line between writers and would-be writers. A writer will put up with the pain, the anxiety, and all the crap to get what they want, which is their development as an artist. Whenever it's a choice between ego and information, the ego has to go to the side. It's about the good of the story, not the massaging of ego.

Kate Braverman could always spot something that had not been thought through in a deep way. I remember her response to a short story that I had worked really hard on: "You know, you could be a romance writer. I hear they make a lots of money!" I went outside and sat on the curb and cried. But, so what? She was a wonderful teacher. Idiosyncrasies don't really matter on that level.

Q: Tell me about the rejection you once got from Joyce Carol Oates, which was a big turning point in your career.
A: Because Joyce Carol Oates has had a huge impact on me as a writer, I used to send everything I wrote to the *Ontario Review,* where she is associate editor. I always got just flat rejections from the *Ontario Review,* but never say die.

I wrote a long story, about forty pages, called "White Oleander." I sent that story to her, and I got back, a one-inch-square yellow Post-it note, saying, "Much strong writing here, but the story is far too long for OR. First chapter of a novel? JCO." And, you know, my God! You talk about a good rejection! Joyce Carol Oates thinks this could be a novel! I had not thought of writing a novel from that story, but I immediately thought, "Why not?"

Q: Why do you think it took ten years to sell your first short story?
A: It was due to a couple of misunderstandings, one of which was, "Send to the places you read." I don't think so! I don't think a new writer is going to get published in the *New Yorker!* That was a *huge* mistake. But I didn't *know* any writers. *Poets & Writers Magazine* was my only link to the world. I didn't know *not* to send to *The New Yorker.*

My first mistake was sending stories to the wrong places, and the second mistake was following the strictures of "Submit one at a time." Submit the story to *Dogbreath Review,* and then you have to wait till you get your rejection before you can send it on to *Left Armpit Gazette.* I've had arguments with journal editors about this. They're looking at this tidal wave of submissions from their point of view. But if you think of it from the writer's point of view, you might wait six months to get one rejection. If you get fourteen rejections on a story before it's accepted, which is pretty normal, that could be *years.* And I think that that's just brutal.

Q: As a beginning writer, you had no contact with other writers?
A: No. I majored in history, and I didn't know any writers. Then I decided I wanted to write fiction, and I just started writing. By the time I knew there was such thing as an MFA program, I had already started my life. I don't think my husband would have dropped everything and moved to Iowa.

Q: Tell me about the first short story you sold.
A: It was published in the journal of the UCLA Extension program, *West/ward* in 1990. Then I had a young adult novel that

sold in 1994. I had a party, and I put all of my rejection letters on the walls and they reached from the living room baseboard to over my head—on all four walls.

Q: Were any of them especially memorable?
A: One was from a publisher rejecting that same Young Adult novel as being too old for them, too stereotypical, too this and that, and we've seen this before. Then, after the book came out and got decent reviews, I got a letter in the mail from a publisher saying how much he admired the work and how courageous it was, and exciting, and the character development was good, and blah, blah, blah. Sure enough, that was the same publisher that had rejected the book.

Q: Amazing!
A: I was hysterical. I always wanted to frame those two letters together, so students could see that rejection doesn't mean a thing. Stories or books can sell for reasons that you can't even imagine. The mother in the story is Hungarian, and the editor's mother was Hungarian. You don't know what it is that's going to do it.

This was another rejection for that young adult book: "Sorry, but this isn't the kind of thing we're looking for. Please send me the stories about good, clean wholesome kids who learn something about themselves or life that makes them stronger and happier but not bitter because they don't need to be bitter."

Q: How do you keep from being bitter?
A: Well, you know, it got to the point—maybe year eight or nine—that I realized that I could write for the rest of my life and never sell anything, ever. I had to ask myself, What do you do? Do you keep working, or do you just throw in the towel?

And I realized that you don't need anybody's *permission* to write. If, on my deathbed, I can look back and I say, "I did what I wanted to do in life," no one can take that away from me.

Rejection can't take that away from me. You don't need to be published, you don't need to be accepted, you don't need anybody's seal of approval to do it.

When I started writing, I did it for all kinds of reasons—making a mark, and showing people, that kind of thing. But after eight years, I realized there are other reasons. I don't know what I think about things until I write about them. I don't know who I am until I explore myself in that way. I need to write on a deep psychological level. I couldn't give that up.

Q: So even if White Oleander *hadn't done so well, you would still be writing?*
A: Absolutely. When you write a book, you don't know if anybody is going to be interested in it. Even when *White Oleander* was done and we sent it out to editors, I kept thinking, "Who the hell is going to care about this, except me?" But when you as a writer care, that's when you make others care. Much moreso than looking over you shoulder and wondering what will sell.

Q: Do you have any unpublished novels?
A: I have several in the file cabinet. They are deeply in the file cabinet and they will not see the light of day.

Q: Why haven't you sent them out?
A: You know, when my daughter was about eight, she found some artwork of hers from when she was in kindergarten, and she was trying to "fix" the pictures. I told her, "These are your pictures from when you were five. They are an example of who you were then. Now you do something else, because you're eight."

I feel that way about my old books. That's where I was at that stage in my development as a writer. I have no interest in trying to fix them and get them out. And inspiration is constant. You don't use up your ideas. There's always something more to write.

Q: Do you feel any affection for those old works?
A: I do. They're like kindergarten pictures. I have great affection for them, but they don't really represent me at my best.

Q: How long did it take you to sell your first novel, Kicks?
A: After four years, I thought I would never sell it, and I told the agent to withdraw it. Instead, he just stopped sending me the rejection letters.

Q: That was smart of him!
A: The thing about agents is, they don't have the attachment to the work, so it doesn't rip them up when they get a rejection.

Q: What happened with White Oleander?
A: I was not prepared for a sale within six months. That was not what I had pictured would happen. The fact that it sold at all was a huge thing. The fact that there was a first printing of forty-five thousand copies was a huge thing. Then Little, Brown got behind the book and the booksellers started to talk about it. All *that* was just more than I had imagined. So for it to be picked by Oprah Winfrey and become a big bestseller was so unimaginable that it took me many years just to be able to believe it had happened.

Q: Did that success had any impact on your ability to write the next book?
A: Oh yeah! At first I was in total denial: It would just be work as usual, no big deal. Psychologically that is just very thin ice, to believe that. It *does* have an enormous impact, and it takes a while to absorb. It's like Alice in Wonderland's "Drink Me." You get huge, and then you get microscopic. It takes a while to come back to normal size.

Q: How did you finally settle back down?
A: I worked for quite some time on a book that never came

together, and then I started working on something else. Now it's coming really well. But I had to get out of the Godzilla stage, and then I had to get out of the one-celled-organism-that-doesn't-deserve-to-live stage, and to finally come back to normal size.

Q: Don't you feel secure at this point in your career? At least you know that people are going to read what you've written.
A: But if my next book is not good, then what will I do after that? There's no such thing as a permanent state of grace.

I tell my students that anxiety is at least eighty percent of writing, and that if you cannot tolerate a fair amount of anxiety in your life, then you can't be a writer. As you're writing, you don't know what's going to happen. You don't know if it'll work out, you don't know if it's going to be accepted, and a lot of people can't live with that. I think the uncertainty is one of the hardest things about writing.

Q: Do you have a hard time dealing with negative reviews and criticisms?
A: Just like any other critique, it depends on how true they are. All books will have flaws; we're humans, not angels. If somebody sees the flaws that you weren't able to solve, that always hurts.

The reviews that don't upset me are when it's just a matter of taste. I write a long sentence. I work off imagery and metaphor. Some people really, really don't like that kind of writing. Just like some people like chocolate and some people would rather have strawberries.

Q: You once said that you originally became a writer because you felt ignored.
A: Writers write because we're forcing people to see the world the way we do.

That's especially true of those of us who were told in childhood, "Nobody cares what you think." I heard that said many a time when I was a child.

Q: That is such a powerfully awful statement!
A: We don't become artists because we have great childhoods.

Q: Speaking of, does your daughter have any desire to be a writer?
A: When my daughter was in nursery school, they went around in circle time and asked the kids what they get in the mail. One kid said, "We get a letter from Grandma!" and one kid said, "We get a catalog." My daughter said, "We get rejections." At three, she already knew what the writer's life was like. She'd seen her mom go to the mailbox and just start to cry. So she's not interested in becoming a writer.

That is the writer's life. People who read books that *did* get published and stories that *did* get published don't understand that you get rejected more than you get accepted. Or that for every story in a literary journal there are a hundred people who went to their mailboxes and started to cry.

Q: Has your relationship with your writing changed since White Oleander *was published?*
A: It's changed a great deal. I don't worry about publication, so that's a huge area of anxiety that is gone. The constraints on my time are very different. I don't have to have a job, so I can work a longer day without interruption. It's very much more just me and the work, which is really nice.

And people treat you differently. It used to be, I'd get calls from other moms, "Oh, are you working? Can you take Bobby?" The idea that you're a writer and working at home is something of so little respect. But once you have some success and somebody calls, "Are you working?" "Yes." "Oh, wow!" People who normally would not listen to you for thirty seconds are now listening to you with great respect. And you try not to have a chip on your shoulder about it.

Q: But isn't that your dream come true?
A: Yeah. But because of all the suffering, it's hard to accept it. We

know how to be failures! Our the defense mechanisms are in place. But we don't know what to do with success.

Q: Then again, everybody wants to have that problem.
A: Right. I mean, I'd rather have that problem, too!

ARTHUR GOLDEN

BERND AUERS

"You have to remind yourself that it's very hard work.
If you drift along thinking you've got some sort of gift,
you get yourself into real trouble."

When Arthur Golden's Memoirs of a Geisha *appeared on the best-seller lists in 1997, it looked as if a new literary talent had appeared out of nowhere. The* Washington Post *called the book "a breath-taking performance twice over, once by its bewitching central fig-ure; and once by the masterful puppeteer who has given her life," while the* New York Times *admired it as "a finely observed picture of an anomalous and largely vanished world."*

Little did anyone realize how long Golden had struggled with that book—ten years of researching, writing, rewriting, re-researching and rewriting yet again, adding up to 2,300 raw manuscript pages.

Arthur Golden was born in 1956 in Chattanooga, Tennessee. He presently lives in Brookline, Massachusetts, with his wife and two children.

Q: Memoirs of a Geisha *was a huge success, but initially it was rejected in a big way. Can you tell me that story?*

A: Yes. When I first wrote the book, it was very different than it is now. I wrote it as a third-person narrative told from the point of view of an adult.

Six years into the project, I thought it was time to start hunting for an agent. I called around, got some names, and sent out some queries. Eventually, my phone rings, and it's a hot-shot editor who says she'd love to see the book, and offers to put me in touch with an agent.

So I call the agent at the editor's recommendation, and we have a very nice conversation. I tell her that I'm planning to come to New York in about a month, and that I'll mail her the manuscript. Then I wait and I wait and I wait.

Two days before I'm due to leave for New York, the phone rings. The agent says, "Well, you certainly do know how to write. I think what you should do is call the editor and make a lunch date with her. Then I want you to come and see me right afterwards, because you're going to have a number of options."

So of course I get so excited by this that I walk around the block unable to concentrate on anything, just beaming.

When I get to New York, there's a message that I should call the editor's office. It turns out that she's not going to be able to have lunch, and that I should really talk to the agent first.

The agent tells me, "Arthur, this is not the manuscript I was expecting."

I say to her, "Wait a minute, you *read* it."

"No, I didn't read it."

"What was the comment, 'You sure do know how to write?'"

"Well, you do know how to write, but this was not the manuscript I was expecting."

So I say, "Gee, I'm surprised to hear this because of what you told me on the phone the other day."

"Well, the editor called me and felt the same way."

So I ask if she can tell me what the problem is with the manuscript, and she says she doesn't know what to say except that it's dry. It isn't the characters, or the dialogue, or even the story—just the way it's written. The editor, she says, felt the same way.

"It could be a best-seller," she tells me, "but not the way it's written here."

Q: *Did you ever find out why you got the run-around like that?*
A: It wasn't until later on that I figured out what must have happened. The agent had not bothered to read the manuscript, figuring that the editor was going to buy the damn thing anyway, and there was no point in her wasting her time, considering all the stuff on her desk. It wasn't until she got a call from the editor saying, "Wait a minute, have you read this?" that she actually sat down and read it.

Q: *Meanwhile, what did you do after that last conversation with the agent?*
A: Well, I went home, not having had my best day. I had nothing else to go on but those comments, and I decided that I'd made a mistake writing the book in the third person from a very remote perspective. I decided to rewrite it in the first person from a child's perspective instead of an adult's.

Honestly, the idea of having a best-seller is not what prompted me to go back and rework the book. It was rather that everybody seemed to find the manuscript dull, and I had not intended to write a dull book. I'd been attracted to this material because it presented such terrific possibilities! If it was dull, I knew I must have done something wrong.

Q: *Did you bring the rewrite to the same agent?*
A; I was planning to. Then, when I was finishing the rewrite, I found out I was being audited by the IRS. They said that since I had no income from writing, my writing was a hobby, and I couldn't deduct all the expenses that had gone into writing the book.

I called that agent and told her about the new manuscript, and I also asked if she would write a letter to the IRS on my behalf. I wrote up a draft of a letter and faxed it to her. Two or three weeks later the agent wrote back saying "I really don't feel comfortable doing this. Perhaps you should call the editor." So I did, and she refused, too.

My accountant wasn't pleased. He said, "You don't know how bad this is, because I've already told the IRS that a letter was on its way." As it turned out, I wasn't allowed to deduct my research, including most of the expenses of my trips to Japan. Since then I've paid so much money to the IRS in taxes I can't tell you.

A friend of mine put me in touch with another agent. The new agent was enormously enthusiastic and signed me up, and we've worked together ever since.

Q: If you had given up when that first agent and editor rejected you, Memoirs of a Geisha *would have just died instead of becoming what it became.*
A: It certainly would have. Because what I'd written before was in no way this book. It all goes to show that you never know where life's going to lead you.

Q: That's for sure. I never thought my first book would be about rejection, instead of a bestselling novel. By the way, is that first agent still out there?
A: Oh, yes. I haven't spoken to her again since that time, but there's no way she could *not* know about this book.

Q: Is there a kind of vengeance there?
A: Every so often the thought does give me a kind of secret satisfaction.

Q: When my work is rejected, I usually go through a period of despair before I am ready to rewrite. Is that the way it happened for you?
A: I remember that I was very upset. The thoughts that went through my mind included, "Should I ditch this thing and try to get a job somewhere?"

It was not the first time I had heard that the book was dry. But I'd heard it before only from people who didn't have any influence over my future. To hear it from professionals in publishing felt to me like something I should really be listening to.

I had been thinking about writing the book in the first person for some time, and this felt like a solution I could get excited about. So literally within an hour of the rejection, I was already thinking about that. I didn't go through a period of utter despair where I really couldn't think, but I certainly wasn't happy.

Q: There's an interesting psychology involved in getting from point A—the rejection, to point B—the decision to rewrite.
A: I'm sure it has to do with believing in yourself. If you allow yourself to feel overwhelmed by the rejection, you're in bad shape. If you can say, "OK, this didn't work, but I know that I can do this," that makes it a lot easier.

Q: Why do you think rejection hurts writers so much more than other people?
A: If you're trying to peddle snow shovels, you don't feel like a snow shovel in some fundamental way represents you. Whereas when you go out with a manuscript, it has a different meaning.

Q: Much different. It's harder to separate the self from the manuscript.
A: Well, that is the problem. That is the challenge of writing fiction.

Q: You've just sold your second novel to Knopf. What can you tell me about it?
A: It's quite a different story from *Memoirs of a Geisha*. It's about a guy who starts in Amsterdam and comes over to the United States in the mid-1800s. He becomes a successful businessman in the meat-packing industry.

Q: *I guess there's not much point in speculating on how you would have felt if it had been rejected.*
A: Well, I don't know how anybody could handle that well. And I'm not talking only about rejection. It would be hard even if the book were taken, but taken unenthusiastically.

Q: *What do you do to keep yourself from worrying about things like that while you're writing?*
A: It's funny, but I do find that it is so much easier to stay withdrawn from the world. Here in my study, it's just me and my work. I don't have to put up with the hassles of, What did somebody think about it? Is it going to sell well? Are people going to like it? And even though it's very difficult, it's also very satisfying. So I guess one of the ways of dealing with the difficulties that surround the problem of rejection or people's feelings about your work is just to keep yourself in your study.

Q: *You mean, hide?*
A: No, not hide. Focus on different things. But you can only really do it once you know you're on the right track. The problem is, how can you know if it's really working? I think a great deal depends on developing your technique.

Q: *How so?*
A: Writing is like a conduit; you put something into it, and on the other end it's taken out without your presence. You can't be there to say, "No, no, no, no. I didn't mean it like that!"

There is always a gap between what you want to say and what the reader understands from the thing you've written. As you're writing, it's very difficult to know what the reader at the other end will take away. It's not the issue of how a word might resonate; those things actually can be pretty easy to predict. It gets a little fuzzier when you're talking about a character—will this character be empathetic to the reader?

And at the larger level—the level of the movement of the

narrative, the involvement of the reader in events, how the events do or don't affect the reader emotionally—those things can be the most difficult of all to predict. The only approach is to develop your technique so you know you understand the mechanics of a story, that you understand the role the characters play in the story, and that you understand the importance of the narrative.

Q: *How do you know when you've reached that point?*
A: I guess you never really do. It's a lifelong process. But as long as you can see that your understanding improves year by year, you're on the right track.

Q: *It takes such a long time to learn to be a novelist!*
A: I always hear these stories from people, "I wanted to write a novel, so I quit my job and went to a cabin in the mountains. At the end of the year, I realized I have no talent." That's a very sad story, because one year is not enough time. It's not that they don't have enough talent, it's that they haven't given it a chance!

I tend to be very analytical, and I break fiction down into discrete elements like descriptive prose and dialogue and characterization. When I wrote the first two drafts of *Memoirs of a Geisha*, there was one thing I missed completely: narrative structure, the development of the story. If you don't present the material in the right way, it's likely to fall flat. Only if all the elements have been constructed properly will it work. For me, that's what separates the first two drafts from the third one.

Q: *Is it scary, writing a second novel after such a successful first novel? Do you worry that people are going to say, "Where are the kimonos? This isn't what we wanted at all?"*
A: What I worry more about is, the book has been very difficult to write. But I think it's best to worry more about doing the hard work than about how people will respond.

Q: *If you worry about people liking it, the work can be ruined.*
A: It's paradoxical. The more you put yourself at risk as you write, and the more personally you involve yourself with the work, the greater the chance that it really might be good. But also the worse your reaction will be if the work is not appreciated.

In some ways I never *stop* thinking about the reader, but the reader probably is me. I sometimes read over a passage—honestly, I'm not kidding—maybe forty times before I'm done with it. And it's not that I sit and read it over and over again. It's that I write four sentences, maybe even three sentences, than I go back and read it all over again to see if whether those two sentences seamlessly move the thing in the direction I'm trying to take it.

Now if it's a simple scene of people sitting around the dinner table, and I know exactly where the conversation is going to go, that's much more straightforward. But when you're dealing with a kind of an emotional realization that a character comes to, or a reflection and a sudden association that a character makes between something in the past and something that has just happened, those things can be very, very difficult. I find that I have to read those things over and over again to make them work. In that way I'm always thinking always about the experience of the reader.

Q: *After* Memoirs of a Geisha, *you know that your second novel is definitely going to have an audience. Does that affect your writing process?*
A: It can make it very difficult to write. When you're writing your first novel, you're really worried that you're going to spend ten or fifteen years on this, and then you're going to end up having to go and get a job. You don't have to worry about that with your second novel in quite the same way. But the other part—knowing that it's going to be compared to your first novel, that people are going to be inclined, perhaps, to want to dismiss it—isn't so easy.

For some reason, nobody really cheers for second novels or second achievements. And as you can imagine, that part can be a little difficult. Sometimes it's easier to go run errands than to sit and put yourself at risk in this way.

Q: Do you pay much attention to reviews?
A: Not wanting to read reviews is a kind of protective mechanism. When you sit down to write, you really don't want to hear in your head the voices of critics who say, "Well, the novel dragged." Then you say, "Is this novel dragging? What am I going to do to keep it from dragging?" Pretty soon you're writing in counterpoint to the criticism that's been leveled at your book, and that's just a terrible thing.

Q: Are there any other obstacles in your career that are as difficult as rejection?
A: It's funny, but what can be as difficult as rejection is adulation. Because you have to be very careful not to believe your press. I often think that if I had been able to see the future and know that my book would be taken up by a great many people and read and enjoyed and appreciated, I might have felt a certain kind of infallibility. I wouldn't have done the hard work of struggling to put the thing together.

I think that's what happens to people at a certain point in their career. They think, "I now have a track record, and this is going to be appreciated because people are going to appreciate me." And that's not true. It's not you, it's the hard work you've done.

You have to remind yourself that it's very hard work. If you start to drift along thinking that you've got some sort of gift, and all you have to do is sit at the keyboard and it will all come forth, you get yourself into real trouble. You may not suffer feelings of rejection, but it certainly can be a tremendous obstacle to doing good work.

Q: Do you have any advice for writers who are having a hard time dealing with rejection?

A: I do have one thing, for what it's worth. It verges on the trite, but it's been meaningful to me.

I play classical guitar. One night I was in my music room practicing and everything was going wrong. I was getting ready to put the guitar into the case when I realized that I was there to practice, not to play a concert. If things were going badly, it meant I had to practice more carefully. Because the days when everything goes well are the result of the work you did on those bad days. The work you do on the bad days will determine who you are and what kind of a guitarist you become.

When the manuscript that became *Memoirs of a Geisha* was rejected, I remembered that guitar-practicing episode. I thought, "Here I am in my darkest moment. And what I do now will determine the outcome."

Q: So in writing, as in guitar playing, talent isn't enough?
A: It certainly isn't. The devotion and the willingness to do it and to do it again, and to learn, are the most important things.

JOY HARJO

"You can use rejection to put you in a funk and
stop you from writing, or you can crumple it up and use
it to build your fire in the evening while you write."

*Joy Harjo, a member of the Muscogee/Tallahassee Wakokaye
Grounds tribe, is a poet, musician, writer, and performer. Her
books of poetry include* She Had Some Horses, In Mad Love and
War, The Woman Who Fell From the Sky, A Map to the Next
World, *and* How We Became Human. *She has also written a children's book, a book of poetic prose with photographs, and co-edited
an anthology of Native women's writing.*

*A former member of the National Council on the Arts, Harjo's
awards include the 2002 Eagle Spirit Award from the American
Indian Film Institute, the Oklahoma Book Award for Lifetime
Achievement, the Oklahoma Book Award for Poetry, and the
Lifetime Achievement Award from the Native Writers' Circle of the
Americas. A professor at UCLA in American Indian Studies and
English, Harjo lives in Honolulu, Hawaii. She also plays saxo-
phone, for which she has received an award for Outstanding
Musical Achievement by First Americans in the Arts.*

Q: What role has rejection played in your career as a writer?
A: Rejection has taught me to be resilient. I read a study commissioned by the National Endowment for the Arts which placed poetry next-to-last in popularity. Being a poet in a country in which poetry has no obvious place of respect is bad enough; being an Indian poet in this country compounds the complexity. In the poetry spectrum, what I am doing doesn't fit within a prescribed tradition. Plus in these times of great "patriotism," anything Indian or Native is considered anti-patriotic.

And then I mix it up, by turning the poems into lyrics, adding a saxophone, drum, some jazz, and tribal elements. By the way, jazz was also at the bottom of the NEA popularity list. Being a woman is another strike against you, and being an Indian woman is even worse.

Then there's the age thing. I turned fifty a couple of years ago, and in this country, youth is equated with power. In all of this, I'm going upstream against theories and notions that govern the status quo of contemporary American society.

So, it is stacked. I don't fit neatly into any kind of category. This confers a certain kind of freedom, but it can also be disheartening to try to find a place.

Q: Is there a Native American poetic tradition?
A: Most tribal groups have poetic traditions that are rooted in oral traditions. And most are found in song traditions. All poetry is born from song. Even European poetic traditions are born from this root.

But in these times, oral eloquence or proficiency is disregarded. And in these times it doesn't count in the poetry establishment if your literary allusions are to sources other than European. The European knowledge field is considered the authority, the place to begin and end.

Q: And you don't follow those rules.
A: No.

Q: *So even within poetry, which is already at the bottom of the heap, you're at the bottom of the heap again.*
A: That's hilarious . . . *And* I play the saxophone.

Q: *Yet you've had a lot of success, both as a poet and a musician.*
A: Yes, but behind those successes is a long list of failures.

Q: *You once said that when you began writing, you had a lot of self-hatred. Did writing help you deal with that?*
A: Yes. The initial impulse for writing was to give voice to a larger, more sacred voice, a voice that would override the small, knotted voice of self-destruction. Self-hatred goes against the gift of breath, of poetry.

Q: *Did the writing process cure your self-hatred?*
A: Poetry has led me to an aesthetic of art, as well as an aesthetic of living, and I don't think those two can be separated.

Q: *How did your career as a writer begin?*
A: I started writing poetry when I was twenty-two or twenty-three. A few years later I decided to focus on poetry, and give up painting and drawing as a career. It was a major shift for me, as I come from a family of Creek Indian painters.

Q: *What was your first memorable rejection?*
A: All rejections are memorable!

After my first two books, at the urging of Audre Lorde, I sent *She Had Some Horses* to Norton. I waited and waited for a response. I received a very nice, encouraging letter of rejection. I wasn't devastated because I knew it was a long shot.

Thunder's Mouth Press took *She Had Some Horses*. It has sold over 15,000 copies and continues to sell well. Funny though, the signature poems from that collection were all rejected from *American Poetry Review*, *Prairie Schooner* and some anthologies.

My next manuscript was *In Mad Love and War.* I sent it to Norton and waited and waited and waited. I'll always remember the day my manuscript was returned. It was a few days before Christmas, a cold, dark and slushy day in Denver. That day was a low point. I felt like a failure, and this was punctuated by my shopping cart wheeling off the curb and spilling all my groceries as I fought to open my truck door at the supermarket.

Q: The first time you sent a book to Norton and it was rejected, you weren't upset. The second time, you were. What was the difference?
A: The first time I was not as established in my career. The second time, I was getting there. *She Had Some Horses* had been selling. So when I sent in *In Mad Love and War,* I thought I had more of a chance.

At that point, I felt like quitting. I asked myself, what's the use? But I go through that regularly, and I've come to accept it as part of the creative process. I know that poetry is about the art itself, the spirit of the art, not about all the rest that goes along with it in this society.

My next submission to Norton, *The Woman Who Fell From the Sky* was accepted for publication.

Q: Your persistence paid off!
A: In that case it did. It doesn't always. Sometimes the lesson is different. And you have to keep going.

Q: Have you received any other rejection letters that really upset you?
A: Yes, a painful one, from an anthology. I sent them what I considered my best poems from *She Had Some Horses.* When they returned them, I burned them.

Q: Some people would have burned the rejection letter, not the poems!
A: True. Though, I didn't burn the originals.

Q: *Why did you burn them?*
A: It was a really self-destructive act, looking back at it. I knew they were good poems, and I really didn't want to burn them. I wanted to strike out at what I felt was somebody's misjudgment.

Q: *Did it make you feel any better?*
A: No. It didn't. And I never did that again.

Q: *Whatever happened to those poems?*
A: They wound up in an anthology that the same people published later on. And a lot of those poems became known as classics.

Q: *You don't give up easily.*
A: From when I was a child, I've always liked to read biographies. I'm always curious about people's stories; how they travel on their map of life, from here to there, and how they maneuver. I've noticed, with the people I admire greatly, that what gives them their power and their energy has to do with those difficulties. It's like electricity. If you think about it, the force of electricity has to do with resistance. So I choose to see it that way.

Everything is energy. You can use rejection to put you in a funk and stop you from writing or doing music, or you can just crumple it up and use it to help you build your fire in the evening while you write your next poems. Just like you can use a fire to burn down a house or to cook your dinner.

Q: *Your heritage as a Native American must have also taught you a lot about drawing strength from rejection.*
A: Native Americans were once one hundred percent of the population, and within a few hundred years we were down to one-half of one percent. Those who are left are strong survivors. We've learned how to keep moving.

You can't close your eyes to the past. You have to use it, and acknowledge it, and keep moving. I think the trick is not to play the victim game. And to cultivate a larger vision, in which you look forward a few years, or a few hundred years, and get a perspective, a shape, or a meaning.

Q: In the introduction to the anthology Reinventing the Enemy's Language, *you expressed ambivalence about using English for your creative expression.*
A: Language is at the heart of a larger set of ironies of being Indian in this country. There's a series of contradictions that are always there.

Q: Yet part of your work has been to take that "enemy's" language and make it your own.
A: Right. Which is, I think, what all people do. We're adaptable. That's why we've managed to live so long, despite our known life being destroyed around us. It's similar to the way that the Navajo picked up techniques of weaving from the Pueblos and jewelry-making from the Spanish, and made something quintessentially Navajo from it.

Q: How long have you been playing the saxophone?
A: I started learning in my late thirties. People thought I was crazy. One of my closest advisers, my translator from Italy, basically said, "You're compromising your poetic gift." My counter to that is that poetry and music came into the world together.

Q: What is it like being rejected as a musician? Is it the same as being rejected as a poet?
A: I think it's about the same. It's just rejection, period.

Q: As a musician, though, you're more often out there in front of people. If they're going to reject you, you know it right away.
A: When I first started performing I was terrified. And instead of focusing on those who appeared to respond positively I'd get sidetracked by a sour face. Once, I let an audience member throw me off because he looked totally disgusted. After the per-

formance he came up and complimented me and said he was blown away by it all.

Q: *You can't always read someone's expression.*
A: I'm pretty good at reading expressions, but I'm not accurate when I'm reading through fear or expectation.

Q: *You used to be very shy. How did you overcome that?*
A: Basically by making myself do what I was afraid of doing. And I failed a lot. One of my biggest failures was when I was playing for the Tucson Poetry Festival. It was one of my first music gigs, and I had a panic attack. I stopped playing and I went off the stage shaking. People probably thought it was part of the act or whatever, but I was devastated.

I came to learn two lessons from this. One was that I needed more practice. Two, I was focusing on myself instead of the music. I find that if I focus on the music or the poetry, I'm OK—whether it's playing, or performing on stage, or writing by myself in a room, or dealing with rejection.

Q: *You have to focus on the act of creation rather than on trying to attain perfection.*
A: Yes. It's not about having perfect pitch every second. It's about singing for the pure love of singing, and about the connection between the singer, the music and the audience.

E. LYNN HARRIS

MATTHEW JORDAN SMITH

"If people find something that they're
passionate about, and stick around long
enough, great things can happen."

*E. Lynn Harris was born in Flint, Michigan, in 1955. He gradu-
ated from the University of Arkansas and became a top computer
salesman at IBM despite longstanding struggles with a difficult
family background and conflicted feelings about his sexuality. Yet
it wasn't until he wrote his semi-autobiographical novel,*
Invisible Life, *that he began to conquer a lifelong depression.
Thanks to Harris's salesmanship and determination, his self-
published effort was picked up by Anchor Books in 1994. There
are now more than three million copies of his books in print, and
each of his novels has been a bestseller. Other titles include* Just
as I Am, If this World Were Mine, Abide with Me, Any Way the
Wind Blows, *and the memoir* What Becomes of the
Brokenhearted.

Harris is co-author, with Marita Golden, of Gumbo: A
Celebration of African American Writers, *and has also published
in* Essence *and the* Washington Post Sunday Magazine. *He is a*

member of the Board of Directors of the Hurston/Wright Foundation and the founder of the E. Lynn Harris Better Days Literary Foundation, which provides support to aspiring writers.

Harris divides his time between Fayetteville, Arkansas, and Atlanta, Georgia.

Q: Why did you become a writer?
A: I started writing to quell a lot of loneliness and despair in my life.

Q: It seems like it worked!
A: Most definitely. My new memoir asks the question, what becomes of the brokenhearted? My answer is, that if people stick around long enough and find something that they're passionate about, great things can happen.

Writing has definitely helped quell depression, just like exercise, and medication. I haven't taken medication in years, but there are certain things I know I must do. I exercise, I take care of myself, and the writing definitely helps. If something's going on with me, I just take pen to paper. I can give my problems, so to speak, to a character.

Q: Why do you think it took you so long to come to writing?
A: I never really saw it as a career option. There were no writers to speak of in Little Rock, Arkansas, and especially no writers who looked like me! So even though writing was something that came very naturally for me, there was no reason for me to think that I could be a writer.

I did aspire to be a sportswriter, but then the gay thing got in the way. The idea was that, because you were gay, you wouldn't be able to control yourself around all these wonderful looking athletes, which is so untrue.

Q: Maya Angelou once encouraged you to become a writer. How important was that?

A: It was very important, because back then I still didn't think that it was a possibility.

Q: *How did you meet her?*
A: She came and spoke at a company where I was a salesman. Being the only black salesman, I got to escort her, and I shared with her. It was the first time I had really voiced the idea of being a writer. She told me, "You must do it, and you must write every day—even if it's just one word."

Q: *Did you follow her advice from that moment forward?*
A: I wish I could say that I did! It's very good advice, and advice that I pass on to other writers.

Q: *What responses did you get from the publishers when you first tried to sell your first novel,* Invisible Life?
A: Oh, the standard, "Thank you, but it doesn't fit into our marketing plans." No real constructive criticism. I think the thing that bothered me most is that sometimes the manuscript would come back, and I could tell that nobody had read it. I sent it out on really fabulous paper, and you could tell when pages had been turned. And that wasn't happening. My heart would sink every time I would get my manuscript in the mail.

The most encouraging letter came from the secretary of an agent who had rejected me as a client. When I called her, of course the agent wouldn't take my call. But the secretary asked the name of my manuscript. Then she said, "Oh, I read it, and it was great. Don't give up. You'll find a publisher."

Q: *How many publishers did you send the manuscript to?*
A: At least twenty-five.

Q: *At what point did you decide to publish it yourself?*
A: Probably after an agent—who now has admitted in public that she really regrets it—rejected me twice. I was afraid of the

depression returning if I sat around and worried about people not wanting to publish me. My thinking was, "Keep moving."

Q: Back in 1991, not many people were self-publishing.
A: No, and a couple of people I talked to tried to discourage me. They said I would be looked upon as a pariah in the publishing industry.

Q: How did you get started?
A: I bought a book called *How to Self-Publish* at a Kinko's copy shop, and I read it from cover to cover. Then I put a plan in place.

Q: Were there any disappointments along the way?
A: Well, bookstores not beating my door down to carry it. Just the overwhelming feeling of having five thousand books sitting in my office.

Q: How did you decide where to sell the book?
A: I would go anywhere, to anybody who wanted to give me a book party. I started taking the books to beauty shops. I did a lot of Black Expos [African American trade shows]. I'd be there two days, and I'd be lucky to sell fifty books.

Q: How much did your background in sales help you?
A: A whole lot. I was trained at one of most successful marketing companies in the world. I'm not afraid to get in front of people and talk. And even though radio stations and newspapers were not really interested in picking up my calls, I was persistent. I was of the thinking that, if I had to go door to door, I was going to get rid of those books.

Q: As a salesman, had you developed any special techniques for handling rejection?
A: I didn't like rejection in sales, but at least I knew that it wasn't

the end of the world. And I knew there was always somebody else out there.

I would also give a lot of myself. By that I mean I would develop relationships with my clients, which made it harder for them to say no to me. Or if they said no, they would tell me the reason why.

Q: *Now you put the same effort into building relationships with your readers.*
A: Right. My relationships with the people who buy my books are very, very important. I answer e-mails from fans every day.

Q: *Your first break in selling* Invisible Life *was when one person bought a hundred copies.*
A: That was Dr. [Henry] Masters, who ran an AIDS program [in Pine Bluff, Arkansas]. He thought the book would help shatter some of the stereotypes the African-American community has about AIDS.

The next big break was at a beauty shop in Atlanta. This guy who came to my first book party as an uninvited guest liked the book so much that he wanted to sell it in his beauty shop. Then a reporter from the *Atlanta Journal-Constitution* came to that beauty shop to get his hair cut—and he ended up doing a big profile on me.

Q: *How did you find an agent?*
A: A young lady saw me delivering books on the loading dock at one of the big bookstores. She looked at the book and saw my picture, and she said, "Oh, you're the author."

I said, "Yeah. I'm the author, the deliveryman, the accountant, everything. I'm a one-man operation."

She said, "Why isn't your agent helping you with this?" And she gave me an agent's name. I contacted him, and of course I got the standard, "We're not taking new clients now." But I became kind of friendly over the phone with his assistant, and the assistant read the book. When I was in New York, he suggested that the agent read it, and the next morning he called me. I was on my way back to Atlanta, and he asked me to come by his office before I left. By then his whole tune had changed; he was trying to sell *me*.

Now, an interesting thing had happened maybe a month before. This lady had called me out of the blue, and she said, "Hey, I'm So-and-so from Doubleday, and somebody gave me a copy of your book, and it was one of most enjoyable weekends I've had in a long time." And she said, "What are you doing now?"

I said, "I'm trying to sell the book."

She said, "Well, if you're ever in New York, look me up." I got her name and number with no clue of what her job was.

So I was getting ready to leave the agent's office, and I said, "About a month ago, this lady from Doubleday called me. She's probably a secretary or something, but maybe she could help us."

When I told him the lady's name, he started to laugh. He said, "She's no secretary, she's the most powerful woman in publishing!"

Q: It seems as if you never doubted from the very beginning, that somehow Invisible Life *was going to sell.*
A: Maybe I was stupid enough not to know. But I felt like I had written a book that hadn't been written before, a book from my heart.

Q: What do you think would have happened if you hadn't gotten that first publishing deal? Would you have kept going?
A: Yes. I would have kept self-publishing my books. I was just so happy with what I was doing, I never wanted that feeling to stop.

Q: If you had to choose between your readers and reviewers, I'm guessing you would choose readers.
A: Right. Because a reviewer is usually someone who wants to be doing what I'm doing.

Q: After you got your first publishing deal, did you stop worrying about rejection?

A: You know, I try not to think about it. I mean, I have three hundred thousand fans who will buy anything I write. I could sit up and say, "Well, Terry McMillan has a million, why can't I get some more of that million?" But I don't think along those lines. I'm grateful for the fans I have, and grateful for the people who want to read my work, and that's it.

Q: Early in your life, you struggled with your identity as a homosexual. And yet, putting that identity into your writing is a big part of what has made you so popular. It's sort of ironic that . . .

A: . . . the thing I was most afraid of gave me this wonderful career.

Q: And the thing that you were afraid of being rejected for, is the thing that got you accepted.

A: Right. I'm accepted now on so many different levels. I get invited to a lot of straight parties and big events in the black community, and I could feel like a token, but I don't. I know that heterosexual men and women genuinely like my candor and honesty.

Q: With all the success that you have now, do you still worry about the depression coming back?

A: You know, depression is like the black dog who can always show up. I just try to fight it off.

Q Meanwhile, it sounds as if you're having a good time.

A: I am. I wouldn't trade my life with anybody.

Q: Do you ever advise other young writers? Do you pass the torch the way Maya Angelou did for you?

A: Oh, definitely. I mostly do mentoring for first-time novelists who have questions about agents and publishers. I've learned a lot from my own agent, and from writers like Terry McMillan who have befriended me and schooled me. So I share that information. For example, a lot of writers don't understand that it takes three or four novels, sometimes five, before you establish yourself. My biggest selling novel was my sixth novel.

Q: What do you tell people who want to self-publish the way you did?
A: I tell them that they have to really believe in the project, and they have to be prepared to work harder than they've ever worked in their life. Because I had fun, but it was hard work. I was doing everything: I had to load the books. I had to be the accountant, I had to mail the books, I had to come up with press releases. I was working sixteen-hour days. You have to have that kind of passion about it.

When writers want to go the traditional route, I tell them to keep sending it out. At some point the right editor will find your manuscript.

Q: Was there any moment in your career when you said to yourself, "Now I know I'm really a successful writer?"
A: When I thought that this had all been worth it, I was on my third book tour. I was in Houston, Texas, at an Afro-American bookstore. I was starting to have nice-sized crowds of maybe seventy-five to a hundred people; whereas on my first tour I was lucky sometimes to get twenty people. This was my first six-figure book, so I was starting to feel like I was making some money.

Anyway, it was a Saturday afternoon, a beautiful day, and after I'd signed all the books, this couple came up. They had a little boy with them—I would say he was nine or ten years old—and he had his head bent down. His parents kind of pushed him and said, "Go ahead and tell him." I never knew what to expect with people, because it was still pretty new. I was used to black women, but I wasn't used to seeing a lot of couples.

The little boy kept his head down. And his father said, "Go ahead, tell him." And he still wouldn't say anything.

So I bent down and got kind of eye level with him. I said, "Is there something you want to tell me?"

He looked up at me—I'll never forget those eyes, he had beautiful eyes—and he said, "I want to be a writer."

Q: Awww. . . .
A: I felt the same way. I said, "Well, you know, you *can* be a writer. I look forward to coming to one of your book signings, just like this."

What touched me so, was not only that little boy, but his parents. They didn't care that I was a gay man. All that mattered to them was that I was a writer, and that I was a black man, and that they wanted their son to see that his dream was possible. And he could know that just by seeing me.

Q: That is such a sweet story.
A: Yeah. Just thinking about it again never fails to cheer me up— and that was so many years ago. I think about that little boy often.

KATHRYN HARRISON

JOYCE RAVID

"Having been dragged through the mud,
I feel like there's nothing I can't write about."

"Trash from the first word to the last." This was just one of the many scathing reviews of Kathryn Harrison's memoir, The Kiss. *The book, which describes the author's four-year incestuous relationship with her father, was vilified both for its controversial content and as a piece of literature. Harrison, who at that point already had three novels under her belt, wasn't surprised to be criticized, but she was shocked at how deeply personal the attacks were. Yet, she says, in many ways the experience made her stronger.*

Harrison lives in Brooklyn with her husband, the novelist and editor Colin Harrison, and their three children. A graduate of the University of Iowa Writers' Workshop who studied English and art history at Stanford University, she is the recipient of a James Michener Fellowship and an artists' fellowship from the New York Foundation for the Arts. Her other books include the novels The Binding Chair *and* The Seal Wife, *and* Seeking Rapture: Essays and Occasional Pieces.

Q: *When did you decide to become a writer?*
A: I don't think I told myself I was going to be a writer until my early twenties. That I became a writer had a lot to do with my husband, Colin, whom I met at the Iowa Writers' Workshop. I started working in publishing in New York right out of the workshop, and at some point he said, "You know, you work so hard on other people's words and you're not getting your own work done. I think that's wrong." Because he exhorted me, I started working on what became my first novel between five and seven in the morning.

Q: *Did you have a hard time selling it?*
A: The manuscript sold with less than minimal pain because I'd been working with an editor who provided liaison with Amanda Urban of ICM [International Creative Management]. At my first meeting with ICM, I was so nervous and lacking in confidence that I fantasized that they had summoned me to discipline me for having been so bold as to think that anybody like Amanda Urban would be my agent. In fact, they immediately signed me up, and they were planning to auction the book on a Monday, but an editor at Random House preempted it over the weekend. So I never had time to worry about its sale. And I'm with that same editor fourteen years later.

Compared to almost anybody else I know, I've just gotten off *so* easily.

Q: *At least until* The Kiss, *a memoir about incest which was hated so intently by so many people. Was that the first time that you were ever really . . .*
A: Savaged? Definitely. I think I had gotten maybe one bad review before that. I was very naive about the media and about many other things as I went into that publication. But when it all shook down, I think that there were as many pros to the experience as there were cons. Even though it was difficult psychically, it also provided some unexpected strengths. It gave me a per-

spective I would not have had otherwise. As much as I've suf-fered, I have no regrets—and I was given a number of things.

Q: *What were you given?*
A: Well, there was a big flap, as you know. It was a book that peo-ple had very strong opinions about. Either they really loved it, or they really disapproved of it and me. The people who hated it were, in some cases, venomous. But of course, I also had people who came to my defense.

One of the things that's very difficult for writers today, is the feeling of being pretty marginal within the whole arena of enter-tainment possibilities. People are always saying that the novel is dying, and that books don't matter. But I published a book that caused a stir, and that was exciting. Some kind of reinforcement came out of that—that it was possible that a book could arrive and people would talk about and argue about it.

Q: *That's a very dispassionate evaluation of the experience.*
A: Well, this was several years ago! Now, having passed through the emotional turmoil, I can regard the whole experience with intellectual curiosity. In the moment, of course, I was stung and shocked and disillusioned.

This might sound ridiculous, but I actually believed that jour-nalists were honorable. I never thought that I'd be quoted out of context, I never thought people would lie to me and misrepresent things that I had said. I didn't understand that people would go for blood, and it also never occurred to me that people would manufacture and publish opinions when they hadn't even read the book. I had to accept that there were a lot of people out there who had negative opinions about me—not because they'd read my work and come to their own conclusions, but because they'd read distortions that had told them how to think about me.

Q: *People criticized you not only as a writer but as a human being, calling you everything from self-serving and narcissistic to irresponsible. They also questioned your right to write the book at all.*

A: I think Jonathan Yardley [of the *Washington Post*] provided the most destructive response. Up until then I'd pretty much managed to keep a stiff upper lip but his review at last made me cry. I felt I'd been treated unjustly in a very public way. It was particularly nasty and humiliating because my husband's parents live in D.C., which is a small, provincial, gossipy place.

Q: *Did you ever have any regrets about publishing* The Kiss?
A: No. I was very clear about why I wrote it, as a human being and as a writer. It was the right thing for me to do, and I don't know what could have convinced me otherwise. The experience politicized me in some ways, because I do think the response had something to do with my gender. I think that if I'd been a guy, it would have been different.

The thing that *really* bothered me was that a lot of people said, either implicitly or explicitly, "This isn't something you should be writing about," or "This is not material that books should be made of." One critic even wrote, in *The Wall Street Journal,* "Hush up." I found that appalling, because I really think that's what writing *is* for. It may not be what cocktail party chatter is about, or what you bring up when you meet a client. But I think books are for talking about what you can't talk about out loud. I think of them as being a corrective in that way. That's why people turn to books.

Q: *The whole thing reeks of censorship, doesn't it?*
A: Well, it wasn't as if I was going to be prevented from saying things. But I found it outrageous that reviewers would say, "You shouldn't be writing about this."

I remember telling Molly Haskell, the film critic, that I'd expected to be protected by whatever quality the writing might have, and the fact that *The Kiss* is not explicit in any way. The topic is inherently sensational, but it wasn't treated that way.

And she just looked at me and said, "You must be nuts. It's *because* it's a good book and *because* it's well written and it can't be dismissed, that people are so angry." Which I thought was really smart, and of course that was also quite comforting, too.

The other thing is this: If you get good reviews all the time, it's possible to get trapped in a kind of "good little girl" box. You publish a book, and you get good reviews, and then you want good reviews again. It's like a report card; you want that little stack of As, and that can be very limiting. Having been dragged through the mud, I think there's nothing I *can't* do now. I feel like there's nothing I can't write about, there's nothing that I would avoid. In that way, it was freeing.

Q: *Were you ever in danger of internalizing what people were saying about you?*
A: I think one editor somewhere in New York, who was quoted anonymously, made a comment to the effect that "Too bad that Kathryn Harrison has revealed this dark secret, because of course now she has dismantled the engine that had driven her writing." And I said to myself, "Oh, wow! That's sort of scary. Is that true?" And five minutes later I thought, "No."

The Kiss was a book that examined a few years of my life, but it wasn't the sum of my life by any means. It was only a fraction.

Q: *And there are plenty of other dark corners and closets in one's life to go into.*
A: Oh, yeah! It's almost unlimited. And then, you could write about somebody else. And there are always novels.

Q: *There's this thing called fiction . . .*
A: Exactly.

Q: *Are you stronger because of the whole experience?*
A: It did probably inoculate me. I realized that I was going to be the kind of writer that some people like, and some people don't.

That's just the way it is. I'm not interested in creating books that everyone embraces or that don't offend anybody.

Q: Has getting ripped to shreds by critics affected your writing process?
A: No. I always did understand that there was only one part of this process that I had control over, and that was the words I put on the page. After I let go of a book, after somebody else has put a cover on it, after other people say whatever they want to say to sell it, and after it is reviewed, it's out of my hands.

I'm always intentionally quite involved in new work when a book is being published. That's my only defense, really. To separate myself and distance myself from the thing that's arriving in the marketplace, and to be completely in love with, and involved with, something new.

Q: And that keeps you a grounded enough to deal with whatever happens next.
A: Yes. Increasingly, my response to being published is to turn my face in the other direction. I'm not going to tell you that I'm somebody who doesn't read reviews. The few reviews that I care about, like the *New York Times Book Review* or Michiko [Kakutani], I'll read pretty closely. But I skim the rest and put them all away, and I've intentionally cultivated a less involved reaction. It can be consuming, and I don't want to be consumed by that.

Q: You want to be consumed by your writing.
A: Exactly. By what I'm working on in the moment.

Q: Is it a wonderful experience, getting your first book published?
A: Your first publication is this great sort of deflowering, and it's shocking. It's not necessarily the benign process that you thought it would be.

As a first-time novelist, you've written this thing—you can't say that it's not you, because it *is* you. Even if it's disguised as fiction, it's *you*. And all work is autobiographical, ultimately. Some writers are a little bit better at disguising it than others, but it's a terribly personal product.

Then it's packaged, and you have all these mostly unrealistic hopes for it. In your mind as a writer, this first publication is a big deal. It's momentous for you. But we live in this ravenous culture that consumes and moves on very quickly.

If you were expecting the publication of your book to be an event, you will be impressed by how much of a non-event it is. Unless you have one of those quite unusual experiences: an unanticipated bestseller. Otherwise, even if you're a solid mid-list writer, your book's published, you get a few reviews, it's out there in the stores, and then, that's that. That's *it!* This is one of the reasons that it's so important to be working on something new.

Q: Because your life doesn't change with publication.
A: No! Not at all.

Q: That's something that isn't talked about enough. Then again, how can you prepare a new author for that?
A: You can't. It's just a process of maturing as a writer. You can't get it until it's happened to you. Birth and children are the metaphors that are usually used for writing. You could explain labor to somebody until you were blue in the face, but until that person had a kid she would never know what you were talking about.

Q: It strikes me that many of your fictional characters are people who are marginalized or rejected by society.
A: That's a valid interpretation. But in terms of my own intent, I think it probably comes out of that consciousness that's pretty common to writers, or any sort of artist, which is that you're a watcher. It can be that you've been marginalized, but it also can be that you've intentionally made yourself peripheral.

You'd rather watch and have perspective than be in the midst of the chaos.

That said, I did grow up in a family that made me feel sort of "other." I lived with my grandparents, my dad wasn't around, and in the time and the place in which I lived, that was unusual. I knew only one kid whose parents were divorced. I didn't know anybody else who was living with their grandparents.

And then, of course, the relationship that I had my with father was something that made me feel deeply different, and completely outside of society. By virtue of that relationship, there was a wall between me and everybody else.

Q: What role has personal rejection played a role in your development as an artist?
A: I am somebody who, from the time that I was born, had to deal with rejection from the one person whom I was determined to make love me, and that's my mother. My whole understanding of myself as a human being grows out of having a terribly destructive, anguished relationship with my mother in which I was rejected repeatedly.

In retrospect, I see myself as a peculiarly hopeful child. I always thought, I always *knew*, that I was *somehow* going to woo her. Somehow I would perform some amazing feat of alchemy and turn myself into a child that she could love.

Of course, that never happened. My mother was really young when I was born, and she was not ready to be a mother. A lot of her dissatisfaction with her life was projected onto me. It didn't occur to me that my mother just didn't want to be *a* mother. I felt she didn't want to be *my* mother, and that if I could turn myself into a different child, then it would be a different relationship.

After the death of my mother, that whole apparatus of making, remaking, revising in order to win love, acceptance, admiration, has been sublimated into my writing. Every time I start a new book, I'm essentially doing the same thing that I did as a child: I'm reinventing myself. As soon as I'm finished with one book I'm already thinking, "Oh, that didn't work. That's not the right one. Let's do this again. This time it's going to work." Then, of course, it's done, I'm dissatisfied, and I start over.

Q: What would happen if you actually were satisfied with a book?
A: Oh, but that will never happen! It can't happen, psychically. I can't look back on anything I've written and say, "That was what I wanted it to be, that was perfect." I can point to passages and say, "That was good." But I'll find another one and say, "Well, that didn't work—that didn't do what I wanted it to do."

What I want has become so mystical and unattainable that, on some level, it's almost a religious goal. I don't mean religious in terms of being a Catholic and going to mass, but it's...

Q: It's like a quest.
A: Exactly. It's the pot of gold at the end of the rainbow, and you never get to the end of the rainbow. I will never arrive at the point where I think, "Oh, this is good enough." I never did with my mother, and I can't *conceive* of it. I can't conceive of getting to a resting point in which I didn't need to reinvent myself again.

Q: Still, there must be some joy in the process?
A: There is. As you know, writing is at least ninety percent drudgery. But when it's going well, I find it to be completely transcendent. I'm lost in it in a way that is satisfying as nothing else is.

There's an old clinical trial that discovered that a pigeon will peck something like a thousand times after having gotten one kernel of corn. You can actually string them along for that long! For me, the thing that writing offers, that moment in which I feel I'm doing it right, is transcendent enough that I'll peck another thousand times.

Q: That's both sad and hopeful at the same time.
A: You know, I still feel tremendously lucky because I think that a lot of people persevere without ever knowing the kernel.

Writing just gives me everything. It gives me my self back in a way that I don't think anything else could. It keeps me from going nuts. And it helps me do something else which is deeply important to me: It allows me to be a good mother. I don't suffer from the illusion that my children are my work. They don't have to be a reflection of me; they can just be themselves. And that's an extraordinary stroke of luck, too.

BILL HENDERSON

LILY HENDERSON

"Rejection helps.
It makes you mad, and you fight back."

Bill Henderson wrote the book on small press publishing—literally. In the early 1970s, after his first novel was turned down, Henderson chose what was then a highly unusual route: publishing it himself. The Kid That Could *never made it big, but Henderson's next book,* The Publish It Yourself Handbook, *did, and his Pushcart Press has had a huge influence on the small press movement in America.*

Henderson also inaugurated the internationally renowned Pushcart Prize, an annual selection of the best of the small presses. The award and an anthology of the winning pieces have helped launch the careers of many grateful authors, including John Irving, Ha Jin, Mary Karr, Susan Minot, and Mona Simpson. In 1998, Henderson edited, with Andre Bernard, Pushcart's Complete Rotten Reviews and Rejections. *He has also written and published* Minutes of the Lead Pencil Club: Pulling the Plug on the Electronic Revolution *and three memoirs.*

Q: Did rejection play any role in your decision to start up the Pushcart Press?

A: Yes—a huge one. I'd worked for many years on my great American novel, *The Kid That Could.* I'd written four manuscripts, as a matter of fact, and I finally had one I felt was really good.

The first time I sent the novel out, in 1968, I got very upbeat comments from something called The Harper Novel Contest. I got a nice personal letter, and I was a finalist, but after that it was all downhill.

Because of that initial nice rejection letter, I kept sending the novel around. I sent it to only one publisher at a time, of course, and I sent it by registered mail, and I waited two months, politely, to get an answer back. Two months later it would come back with a rejection slip. I'd get maybe eight, ten publishers a year to look at it.

At that time there were a lot of publishers; they weren't all conglomerates as they are now. But it was, of course, incredibly frustrating. I'd spent five or six years on this book, and I had put everything I knew into it. So I was in true despair when *The Kid That Could* was rejected. At that time I had no alternatives, really. We had the corporate commercial presses—Doubleday and the rest—and the vanity presses. But there was no small press movement.

So I decided to publish it myself. An uncle of mine ran a little camping magazine in North Plainfield, New Jersey, and I persuaded him to try the book business. We published my novel under the pseudonym of Luke Walton, who is a Horatio Alger character.

Q: How did The Kid That Could *sell?*

A: Lousy. It was reviewed in the *New York Times Book Review*, but it wasn't a great review. I sold five hundred copies. But from that experience, I learned that you could actually publish your own book—and I wanted to tell other people about that. In 1973, while I was working as an editor at Doubleday, I spent my weekends publishing a book called *The Publish It Yourself Handbook*.

That was Pushcart Press's first book. It was a huge hit. It caught on immediately, because there had never been a book like it before. It was reviewed in the *New York Times Book Review*. Victor Navasky, who now runs *The Nation,* mentioned it in a series of articles on publishing in the *New York Times,* and we got four hundred direct orders. We sold about thirty thousand copies. In the twenty-five years since the book first came out, we've sold seventy thousand copies.

That's where rejection led me. I was driven by despair and outrage. If my novel hadn't been so rejected, I wouldn't have learned how to publish books or started my own publishing company.

Q: A lot of people go through the same experience you did, but instead of getting mad, they just crumble. What made the difference with you?
A: Well, if I was going to crumble I was going to go down big time. I was in real bad despair. It was a matter of life or death. I was very, very depressed when the rejections came back. I had spent so many years trying to write the novel, and I loved it. I *still* love it. I still think it's a very funny book. And it's still on Pushcart's list.

Q: As publisher of Pushcart Press, do you use form rejection letters?
A: I know that people who have been rejected find form rejections frustrating. But I do the same thing here at Pushcart, because I haven't got time to tell people I think their book is just horrible. So I say, "My press is very small and we can't do your work." I always blame my press for being so small.

I must admit, I am horrified that I'd hurt somebody's feelings. So I avoid rejecting as much as I can. With the annual Pushcart Prize, we get eight thousand pieces of poetry and short stories each year. I could never possibly respond to all those people, because I'm only one guy in a shack in my back yard. If I find anything that's promising, I try to let the author know. If there's something to give a person heart about, I try to mention it. But if you don't hear from me, you're not one of the three or four books a year that I publish.

Q: It must be gratifying to see how many small presses came up behind you.
A: Yeah, it was gratifying. There was a real need for it.

Pushcart wasn't the first small press, by any means. There was Allen Ginsberg and *Howl* and City Lights and all that, in the forties and the fifties. And of course in the thirties Virginia Woolf was published by Hogarth Press, and James Joyce's *Ulysses* came out from a press in Paris. There were always small presses here and there, but there was never a movement of any sort.

The movement really grew terrifically after *The Publish It Yourself Handbook* came out. Not just because of my book, but because in the sixties people were very active, and in the seventies it just continued.

Q: It's amazing how many good things end up coming out of rejection.
A: Exactly. Of course, that doesn't solve the problem of rejection. Once you're a publisher publishing books, you are rejected by reviewers. That's why I published *Pushcart's Complete Rotten Reviews and Rejections.*

Q: When a book you've published is rejected by reviewers, does that feel as bad as it does when a book you've written is rejected by publishers?
A: Almost as bad. It's dangerous to the small publisher, too, because you sell your books through the reviews. *Publishers Weekly, Library Journal, Kirkus, Booklist*—these four reviews are absolutely crucial. If one or two of them trash one of your books, you could lose your entire bankroll. This has happened a

few times in the thirty years that Pushcart has been around. So if you're rejected by a reviewer, it's doubly dangerous. You lose sales *and* you lose heart.

Q: Tell me how you came up with the idea for Rotten Reviews *and* Rejections.
A: People spend a lifetime writing books, and if they're fortunate enough to get them published, if they survive the rejection slips, then they've got to survive the reviewers. And the reviewers have a very unfair advantage. They can knock something down in an hour, in a couple of minutes, and throw somebody's lifetime into the trash. Then everybody thinks, "Oh yeah, there's a lousy book," which may not be the case at all. It might be a great book. But the only access to the public is that review. So it goes down in history.

That's why *Rotten Reviews* came out. I was so furious that I decided to have some fun. *Rotten Reviews* is supposed to be a funny book. It makes fun of people who criticized the classics. I gave the reviewers their historical just desserts.

Q: That's great revenge.
A: Not only that, but the book was a huge hit. When I published *Rotten Reviews*, I thought, "Oh, Jeez, Henderson you've gone over it now. Reviewers are going to see you're hacking them, and you've had it. They're going to go after *you.*"

But the exact opposite happened. The reviewers loved it, because they could have fun laughing at *other* reviewers. The book was written up in *Publishers Weekly* and featured in the *New York Times Book Review.* Penguin bought the paperback rights and *Rotten Reviews* spent a week on the *Washington Post* bestseller list. So I wasn't made to pay the price, after all.

Q: In addition to getting a good laugh, do you think people got inspiration from the book?
A: I hope so. I hope it makes them feel that they're not in this

alone, which is a big thing when you're in trouble. And I hope it's been healing, in the sense that laughter heals.

Q: *Let's talk about your pre-Pushcart career. How long were you with Doubleday as an editor?*
A: I was only at Doubleday a year and a half before I was unceremoniously thrown out.

Q: *Why?*
A: I just didn't take the place very seriously, I guess. And of course they didn't take *me* seriously. They gave me the old heave-ho.

Q: *Did you learn anything about publishing when you were there?*
A: Yeah. How to hate committees and bigness and business. It's the way things get done, but it wasn't for me.

Q: *So getting fired by Doubleday was probably a blessing in disguise, too.*
A: That rejection was a true blessing, because I was able to devote myself full-time to Pushcart Press.

Q: *Are you still writing fiction?*
A: No. I write memoirs now. One of the latest is *Tower: Faith, Vertigo and Amateur Construction*, about a tower I built in Maine.

Q: *You sent that book to a publisher rather than publishing it yourself?*
A: Yes, I did. Although I would have printed it myself if I had to.
When a memoir is complete, I send it out and see if anyone wants it. Then, if they don't, the hell with them—I've got my own publishing company!

Q: *It must help a lot to know that somehow or other it's going to get published.*
A: That's right. There's no speculation. I've got a publishing company. And everybody does, if they want to be a publisher.

Q: As the editor of Minutes of the Lead Pencil Club: Pulling the Plug on the Electronic Revolution *how do you feel about things like e-books and publishing on the Internet?*
A: Well, I'm not going to knock it entirely, but I think ninety-nine percent of it is nonsense. I believe it's very dangerous for a writer not to go through some kind of pressure cooker in getting the work around; not to go through an editor, or many editors, and rejections—again, it comes back to rejections.

If you want to put your work in a machine and send it out to the world, you don't have any time to reflect on it and think about it. It takes time for the writer to determine if the work is any good. You have to get away from it and get distance. Maybe in five years, ten years, you come back and look at it and think, "That's pretty good," or "That's crap." That's one of the wonderful things about sending stuff around and getting rejected, is that you gain time to look at it again.

The fact that I still love the novel that I published myself in 1973 is important to me. I still think it's good. It still makes me laugh out loud. But I've also written certain other books . . . There's one that I took to the dump. I was ashamed of it. It was embarrassing. It was morally objectionable. I didn't want anybody to ever see it.

Q: And if you had posted it on the Internet, you could have never taken it back.
A: That's exactly my point. It's very easy to get carried away with your own fiction and think, "This is great stuff." Well, a lot of times that's not true.

I've always wondered why this culture is so enamoured of speed. Speed is the enemy of the author. Because you've got to sit down and think, and that takes time. My objection to the Internet is, it's too easy and too fast. Writers need to take time before they publish their work. If they put the stuff in a drawer for five years and *then* put it on the Internet, I'd understand that. But to just to knock something out and then flash it out to the world is very hurtful for writers.

Q: *Did you create the Pushcart Prize to help rejected writers?*
A: It's not so much rejection, as it is giving the writers who aren't writing commercial stuff a chance to appear in print and to be honored for it. They have no chance to be considered for most commercial magazines. That's the idea behind the Pushcart Prize.

Q: *Many of the winners later became famous.*
A: Hundreds, I guess. Raymond Carver was in the very earliest Pushcart Prize, and Mary Karr had a poem, and even John Irving had a story in Pushcart Press Number 2, called "The Pension Grillparzer." It had been rejected everywhere, and he was very, very grateful. Things like that happen all the time.

Q: *Were you hoping that some of these people would make it big?*
A: No. I don't give a damn if people become famous, because I don't believe in it. I'm very happy when they're appreciated. The big point is that these people get read, because they have something to say. And to encourage them. And now and then they break out into a wider audience.

Q: *When Pushcart Prize celebrated its twenty-fifth anniversary in 2000,* Publishers Weekly *said it was among the most influential projects in the history of American publishing. Does this mean that you're part of the Establishment now?*
A: Jeez, I hope not! Besides, who is the Establishment: Bertelsmann, the German conglomerate? There are only about four commercial trade houses left anymore. They've all been bought up and merged, so who are these people?

Q: *Do most writers who win the Pushcart Prize have experience with rejection?*
A: There are so few places that a serious writer can have their stuff appear, that they're almost all rejected. That's how they come to small presses, and that's how they come to the Pushcart Prize.

Q: *When you notify people that they've won the award, what kinds of reactions do you get?*
A: Well, they're very happy, and I'm honored that they are so honored themselves. It's a pretty big deal, and I think that's amazing. I've also had a lot of help making it a big deal: two hundred contributing editors, and all the editors of all the little magazines in this country.

Q: *Has anyone ever rejected you when you've asked them to be a contributing editor?*
A: Oh, no!

Q: *So you've gone from total rejection to the opposite end of the spectrum.*
A: Well, thank you. Rejection helps, you know. It makes you mad and you fight back. It's helpful.

Q: *Do you have any words of advice for rejected writers?*
A: Just keep on plugging. Don't quit. Don't let your heart break. You might retire for a week or two, or a year, but don't quit. It may be the only thing that's worth it to you. What else are you going to do?

WALLY LAMB

CHRISTINE LAMB

"In some ways, I found success
just as intimidating as rejection."

*Wally Lamb is one author who got a career boost from Bill
Henderson's Pushcart Prize—but if he hadn't absentmindedly
submitted the same short story to the same magazine twice, he
might never have achieved that honor. Lamb has since written
two bestselling novels,* She's Come Undone *and* I Know This
Much Is True *and garnered honors such as a fellowship from the
National Endowment for the Arts and a Writers for Writers
Award.*

*A former high school and college English teacher, Lamb devotes
a few hours a month to a writing workshop for inmates at York
Correctional Institution, Connecticut's maximum security prison
for women. From that experience came the book* Couldn't Keep It
To Myself: Testimonies from Our Imprisoned Sisters, *a collection
of inmate memoirs that shows the power of writing to transform
people's lives. Born in Norwich, Connecticut, in 1950, Lamb now
lives in nearby Willimantic.*

Q: You tell a story at writers' conferences about a rejection that turned into an acceptance. It was also the first time you had a short story published nationally.

A: The story was called "Astronauts." I had started it while I was in a low-residency MFA writing program at Vermont College. I've worked in writers' groups since I started writing fiction. So I'd bring it back every now and then, and they would tell me what was wrong with it *this* time, and I just kept plugging away at it.

Finally, I began submitting it. Every once in a while I'd put the stuff together, put enough nickels in my pockets to make my pants fall down, and go down to the drugstore to copy these things and submit them.

I'd send that story off to three or four different magazines, and it would come back rejected from all of them. I'd lick my wounds for a couple of weeks or so, and then I would try to send it out pretty quickly afterwards to the next four places. That happened for about a year.

Because I'm a crappy businessman, I had forgotten I'd sent "Astronauts" to this one magazine, and by mistake I submitted it again. Lo and behold, after having come back the first time with a polite little, "This doesn't meet our needs at this time, thank you for sending it anyway," photocopied note, suddenly I heard from the same magazine that they were going to publish it!

Q: The publication of that story made a big difference in your career.

A: Yes. That was where my agent-to-be read the story. First I got an agent out of that story. Then, at end of the year, the same story won the fiction prize for that journal, so they flew me out to the Midwest to get my prize. When I came back, I heard from the Pushcart Press that they were going to publish it. So that one story set all these other dominoes falling. What it also did was, it validated me at a point when I really needed it.

Q: I think it's so interesting that the same story was rejected and accepted by the same publication. Do you have any idea why that happened?

A: Well, it was really educational for me. When I went to get that prize, the editor brought me into the office, and he said, "Look around wherever you want."

So I went into the room where the manuscripts are—the ones that come in over the transom from everywhere around the country. I saw those stacks and stacks and stacks of manila envelopes. And the editor explained what happens, which is a sifting process. The first readers are usually graduate students. Then the stories are either pushed to the next step or not, and eventually the senior editors read the stories and make their decisions. So it all depends on who's reading it.

For whatever reason, my story didn't grab the first reader. But I do tell that anecdote when I give readings, because I think it illustrates that part of it is just the luck of the draw. That's also why I try very hard not to personalize rejection. I try to see it as, "The stars weren't lined up for this one, so I'll try again."

That story was accepted at one of two really low points in my career. The other time was right before I got a grant from the NEA. Both of those incidents were so well timed. They threw me a life preserver to hold on to and get to the next step.

Q: Tell me about that second low point.

A: Well, it probably doesn't suit your purposes, but there's a spiritual component to all this.

Q: Oh, but people who are dealing with rejection all the time need spiritual components.

A: It was in the middle of a very difficult time. My mother had had a stroke, and we had taken in the kid who turned out to be our third son—we adopted him, eventually, under difficult circumstances. It had just been a really hard year. I had very little time to write, and the balancing act got a little too much for me. I was kind of thinking of shelving the whole thing as undoable.

We didn't have that much money. But I felt an impulse—it was Christmas season—to get down to the local homeless shelter and donate more money than we actually should have been donating. I brought this little guy, Teddy, down with me, and we rang the bell and we gave a nice check to the nun who runs the shelter.

And the next day—who knows if there's a connection—a woman from the NEA called to say that this fellowship that I had applied for eleven months earlier had, in fact, been granted. That gave me a six-month leave of absence to work on the second novel, *I Know This Much Is True,* and it got me sort of revved up again, confidence-wise.

I'm certainly no poster boy for anybody's organized religion, but the older I get the more I believe in the mysteries of life. I'm a firm believer that we are here for one another. And lots of times if you give, you get back more than you have given.

You're a writer—you know that, too. Of course you start out writing for yourself, but then you revise like crazy, and you pull out your hair, and you drive everybody around you nuts, and your "gift" gets read and sent out to the world. You have no control over what's going to happen. But the letters that I get from readers—that's another gift. How cool is that, that people a) took the time and the effort to read your work and b) were good enough to sit down and write you a response to it?

Q: *Do you seriously think you would have given up writing if you hadn't gotten that call from the NEA?*
A: I don't know. Ultimately maybe not, because as hard as it is, writing gives me something that I need. Teaching does, too, but they're different things. So I'm constantly trying to figure out how to balance both. And I'm a hands-on parent, so that's in the mix as well.

Q: *Tell me how you came to write your first novel,* She's Come Undone.
A: I started *She's Come Undone* at Vermont College, where I was

working with a great writer and wonderful teacher, Gladys Swan. That book started as a short story in about 1983. I had submitted the story to Gladys—it was fifteen or sixteen pages long—and she said to me, "Well, my dear, I think you have a few too many pots on the stove on this one."

I said, "What do you think I should cut?"

She said, "I think you should keep going. Maybe you're trying to tell yourself that you want to write a novel."

Had I known what I was in for, I probably would have gone running and screaming from the room. But I just kept going. I began to worry over that character. I felt very parental toward her. I never know what's going to happen next in the stories I'm writing, so I just kept writing to see if she was going to be OK. It was a long process. It took me just shy of nine years.

Q: Did you have a hard time getting the book published?
A: I'm a great avoider of things, and one of the things I was avoiding was the business end of writing. But as I was coming into the home stretch, I started looking at books about agents. I sent a little package of stuff to a couple of the big New York agents, and I didn't hear for maybe two months. Again, I avoided calling them to inquire if they had read it. But finally I did screw up my courage. They both seemed kind of snotty, like it was an imposition to read my stuff and they would get to it when they got to it.

In the meanwhile, another agent had seen "Astronauts." She wrote to me, saying, "If you are looking for an agent, please give me a call, and by the way do you have anything longer that you're working on?"

What happened was, I finished the book and submitted it to her. She had promised a first look to an up-and-coming editor at Simon and Schuster. With my usual bad timing, I finished the book just when that editor was going into the hospital to deliver her daughter.

At the time, I was teaching at the high school in Norwich, Connecticut. It was actually the last day of the school year. A few weeks earlier, some wise guy had thrown a piece of gum down on the carpet, and for a month I'd been looking at that damn gum getting blacker and blacker. After all the students left, I got a cleaning agent from the janitor. I was down on my hands and knees scraping up the gum, and the phone rang in the class-room. It was my agent saying that the editor got out of the hos-pital with her daughter and said, "I want to buy this book." So that was really something. It was a Cinderella story at the end of almost nine years. And I always think of that gum stain.

Q: How did the book do before it became an Oprah pick?
A: It had a fairly good, modest success for a first novel, and it went from hardcover directly to mass market paperback. But after five years, it had gone to sleep. It had gone off the shelves in the bookstores.

Q: Then it got a wake-up call. How did that happen?
A: Oprah called me on a Friday night. She said, "You know, if this goes the way the first couple of books have been going, you're going to need to get ahold of your publisher tonight or this week-end. Don't wait till Monday morning." Around ten-thirty at night I did track down one of the editors from Pocket Books. They had an emergency meeting on Saturday morning, and they started printing that weekend. I think somewhere around three million copies were sold, thanks to the power of TV.

Q: Did you find yourself overwhelmed by that success?
A: It does sort of knock you off your balance a little bit. Suddenly the world comes to your door and wants more stories, and also wants other things from you as well. In some ways I found success just as intimidating as rejection.

Q: How so?
A: I guess because there's a difference between a writer and a quote "author" unquote. When you become something of a pub-

lic figure, there's the seduction to give yourself away to public appearances, speaking engagements, and writers' conferences. It can become a role that you play: *auteur.*

Writing is such a different thing from that. It's primarily a solitary, humbling activity where you may work all day or all week or all month and not get very far. If you keep saying yes to all these opportunities, then you can give away your writing time.

Also, on behalf of writers everywhere, I was enormously grateful and flabbergasted, and I wanted to share as much as possible. So people would call on the phone and I would say, "Yes, I'll come to your class," and "Yes, I'll come to your book discussion group," and "Sure, I'll come give away the prizes at your school . . ."

Q: And "Yes, I'll be interviewed for a book about rejection!"
A: Well, I do have an index card a friend gave me scotch-taped to my phone, with this little scripted polite refusal.

Q: So you have your own form rejection that you give to people on the phone!
A: Yeah. Sometimes I start stuttering and so forth, but you have to be careful that you're not giving it all away.

Q: After a first successful book, were you afraid that the next book might not do as well?
A: Sure. With the first novel, I had no illusions that it was going to get published. I was just writing it to see what happened to the character, and to see if I could finish the story. But with the second book, I had something different. I had a book contract and I had advance money and I also had a deadline. The publisher said, "In two years, please submit your manuscript."

I started *I Know This Much Is True* with a great deal of difficulty. I had lots of thoughts about returning the advance, that this was just a fluke, that I could just go back to full-time teaching, that kind of stuff. But what happens is, eventually, if you keep working at it, if you keep showing up at the desk—whether you're starting to lose your nerve or not—then eventually you start to immerse yourself in the story. Then, when the story becomes more real than you are, when you're really there inside the story, so that you're not particularly conscious of the room around you, you become invested in a different way. That's when all those demons and all those people with expectations go flying out the door. And that's what you're writing for—that's what I'm writing for, anyway—to get lost in those other imagined people's lives.

Q: You're not writing to meet other people's expectations.
A: Somebody told me one day that if you go on Amazon.com, you can go in and read what people are saying about your book, so I took a look. It was a little scary, actually. What spooked me more than the negative or critical stuff was the very positive stuff. When people say things like, "Oh, he's a brilliant writer, he's a genius," you think, "Okay, now whatever I write has to be brilliant." I think you get really hung up on those expectations.

So what I try to do is stay away from those Amazon critiques, open my office door and chase everybody else out of there except the characters. It all comes back to something Gladys Swan said in the beginning of my writing career. She asked me, "What is it that you want out of this? Why are you writing?"

And I said, "Well, I've always loved *To Kill a Mockingbird*, and every year I pass it out to my students. And boy, wouldn't I love to write something that says something important but that people find readable and discussable and enjoyable!"

Gladys said, "Well, my dear, the first thing that you have to do is to banish from your head any idea of who your readership is. Because if you write your book for yourself, instead of with a readership in mind, then the book will be true. And if the book is true, it will find the audience that is meant to read it." That advice has served me well for over twenty years now.

Q: And now you pass that advice on to your writing students.
A: When I teach writing workshops, I tell the students, "It's not what's good in your story and what's bad, it's what's working in the story and what's not working yet." If you keep mining the material for the potential that's there, then—bam!—you'll get there. That's my advice for writers. I think it's weathering the disappointments, it's persevering, it's revisions, and support. Because we all have those periods of wondering, "Why am I putting myself through this?" If you have a supportive writing community, they can get you through that as well.

Q: What's the worst rejection you ever got?
A: I had one scathing rejection from a very well known national magazine (but not the *New Yorker*). I can't find the actual letter, but twenty years hence, I still remember the gist of it. The editor said that he found the main character unsympathetic, he found the contents of the story off-putting, and he felt that the story had not been resolved in a pleasing way. But other than that, he liked it.

Q: But what's left after that?
A: The opening paragraph? I don't know. But you know, even that was encouraging, because he did say at the end, "Try us again with other stuff."

Q: Do you ever worry about whether you've researched your characters well enough? For example, what if someone with a twin schizophrenic brother were to read I Know This Much Is True *and say, "This is totally wrong?"*
A: With my first novel, *She's Come Undone,* I did virtually no research other than having been a high school teacher and having listened to students' voices all those years. With the second book it was quite different.

I started that story with the voice of a guy who was royally pissed off about something, but I didn't know what. After maybe

135

three weeks, I began to see that his anger was somehow connected to his brother, so I started writing the brother. I wrote a scene between the two of them, and it became clear to me that there was something wrong with the brother, mentally, and that this was somehow connected to the anger.

I grew up in the Connecticut town of Norwich, which housed the largest of our state mental hospitals. I got a tour of the place, and while I was there I buttonholed a doctor. I said, "I've got this guy, he's saying this and doing that—give me a diagnosis for him."

And he said, "It sounds like paranoid schizophrenia." I didn't know anything about it, so I began to read articles and talk to people who have the disease in their family and, in a couple of cases, people who have schizophrenia. I began to gather the research that way, but I didn't stop and learn everything I could about the subject; I kept writing intuitively as I kept building on my knowledge.

Somewhere in that painful six months or so of starting that story in earnest—talk about rejection!—I went to a writers' group meeting at a restaurant. One of the members there, an elderly woman, has a son who is mentally ill.

The first pages of this new novel had been hard in coming, and I was very nervous about reading them. After I'd read seven or eight pages, this fellow writer slapped her notebook shut and stood up from the table. She jabbed her finger in my face and said, "If you're going to take up this subject, you'd better get it right, because there's a lot of crap out there in the culture. You'd better do your homework, because the last thing people with mental illness and their families need is more crap." And then she promptly took her notebook and exited the restaurant. It was a tough moment.

Q: *She didn't throw a drink in your face, did she?*
A: No, but I was mortified! Although ultimately I was very grateful to her. Her voice and that challenge kept coming back to me over and over again, and I did take my research very seriously.

I get a lot of letters from readers of that book, and I haven't gotten any from family members, saying, "You did it all wrong," or "You sensationalized it." The letters I get are grateful that I put the subject on the table and made them feel less alone with their struggle.

Q: It also goes to show that an intuitive character development process really can work.
A: I guess. But it's hard to get to that place, as you probably know. I spend a lot of time helicoptering above a story before I'm actually living in it—and that's the hardest part for me. That's the maddening part, and that's where the fear comes in.

Q: When you haven't quite gotten it.
A: Right. Or when you sort of see it from a distance. I almost always write first person, because it fulfills some kind of a need that I don't really understand to inhabit somebody else's life. It takes me forever to get these novels written, but I come out the other end and I'm changed, somehow.

Q: Do you think you would keep going even if you didn't get published?
A: Now that I've seen how it works, and how it plays into my non-writing life—yeah. I think writing fiction has made me more open-minded in many ways.

The same goes for nonfiction, for example, serving as an editor for *Couldn't Keep It To Myself: Testimonies From Our Imprisoned Sisters,* by the women of York Correctional Facility, where I run a writing seminar. There are all kinds of assumptions that I used to have about prison and prisoners that I cast aside as I worked with the gals in that workshop. They've opened me up in so many ways, too. They've opened me up to things about the justice system that I didn't know, and about the conditions by which people come to prison. I feel grateful to know them as individuals.

Q: Being a prisoner has to be the ultimate rejection.
A: It's not only rejection, but it's also silencing. I think, sadly enough, that prison administrations are giving the public what it wants. And I think what we as a society want is to lock these people up and have them not make any waves, so we don't have to think about them. If we can't see them or hear their voices, then we can keep our denial intact. We don't have to examine conditions like incest, racism, and poverty that land people in prison.

Q: How did you get involved in teaching that workshop?
A: This was one of those situations where I couldn't say no. I was only going to go to the prison once, for ninety minutes. But, to use a bad pun, the women there captivated me. And they've been the most exciting students I've ever worked with.

Many of the women have been victimized all their lives. They are there because of that, as well as because of the criminal act that sent them to prison. After all, if you're told all during your formative years that you're an idiot, or you're whacked across the face for saying that grandpa molested you, you learn silence. So one of the first things that you have to do with incarcerated writers is get them beyond the assumption that they are voiceless.

Q: What happens when that energy is released and they start writing? It must be astounding.
A: Well, it is. That's why it's such an exciting experience.

Prison is a place where nobody trusts anybody much. I'll go down there, and they're thinking, "Why should we commit ourselves to paper for this middle-aged white guy? But then they gradually see that it's not for me, it's for them. And once they start trusting their memories on the page, they begin to feel better.

One of my first students there was a woman who was suffering from post-traumatic stress. She couldn't read her stuff without crying. She would start, and she would break down, and she would pass it to somebody else in the group. Then they would read it and we would have our discussion. She would sit there taking notes, and drawing Kleenex after Kleenex from the box. But writing her memories began to do something for her. She stopped crying and took command of her own work.

I've seen the same thing happen again and again. Maybe the toxic memories become more manageable or more contained on an eight-and-a-half by eleven-inch sheet of paper. I don't know what it is, but I know it makes a difference. The women begin to see that writing makes them feel better than holding it in.

So in terms of the rejection thing, I think that for many of us—but certainly for incarcerated writers or writers suffering from post traumatic stress—self-rejection or rejection of self or the belittling of self, is a huge issue that has to be mastered.

Q: In a way, that's the granddaddy of all rejections. Getting a rejection letter from a magazine is nothing compared to rejecting your own self.
A: Yes.

BETSY LERNER

BARRY MARCUS

"People who are the real thing just keep writing."

Betsy Lerner is one of those rare beings who combines a career as a top literary agent with authorship. She graduated from Columbia University with an MFA in poetry, then spent thirteen years as an editor at Houghton Mifflin, Ballantine, Simon and Schuster, and Doubleday before becoming a literary agent at The Gernert Company in 1999.

Lerner's memoir Food and Loathing: A Lament *describes the personal struggles that accompanied her early life as a writer and editor. Her book* The Forest for the Trees: An Editor's Advice to Writers *is written in a sympathetic, down-to-earth voice that is especially illuminating for writers who have always wondered how the publishing industry really works.*

Q: You have written about a very difficult and personal subject: mental illness. Do most writers fear rejection when they talk about such personal subjects?

A: Certainly people have a lot of fear in terms of bringing their work forward. The fear is based on a lot of different things. One is that they might get rejected. Another is that they might be found out—that people will see more than they wanted them to see. Another fear is losing control as an artist, because the minute you bring something out, it's no longer really yours.

Q: But isn't the fear of being found out tied to a fear of being rejected?
A: For me that wasn't a fear. Once I decided to write about my personal struggles, I came to terms with them.

Q: In other words, the hardest decision is putting the secret on paper? What people think about it afterwards is almost secondary?
A: It *is* secondary. Some writers treat it as primary, often because they are not far enough away from the material. But you really shouldn't care what anybody thinks.

Q: You talk in your book, The Forest for the Trees, *about writers who are seeking parental approval through their writing. Is that one of the reasons writers can take rejection so hard?*
A: Definitely. And whether the writer is seeking a mother's love or a father's love, those rejections resonate. That can be part of a person's drive, to constantly prove herself to an absentee or cold or suffocating parent.

Q: Does that end up being a positive force in the writer's life?
A: I don't know what it would be like to work *without* needing to prove something. It might be amazing. But most people are working out trauma and conflict and powerful emotional histories in their artwork and their stories and their paintings.

Q: Do you think it's risky for an artist to resolve these internal conflicts? Does one have to choose between creativity and psychological wholeness?

A: I think it's crazy not to get help, or to think that therapy will take away your creativity. That's not how it works. It's not an either/or situation.

People who *don't* get help can wind up not producing anything, or quitting. How many people just quit writing or pursuing whatever art they want, and become very bitter!

Q: Was your motivation in writing The Forest for the Trees *to help writers who are in danger of quitting?*
A: It was really motivated by a constant feeling I had when I went to writers' conferences that there are insiders and outsiders, and that if you perceive yourself to be an outsider, you'll never get your work published. I wanted to demystify the way publishing people think and the way the publishing world works.

Also, because I'm a student of psychology, I wanted to write about my observations on how writers' psychology impacts their lives. Are they saboteurs or are they self-promoters? Is their neurosis healthy or ultimately detrimental? I wanted to describe and codify all these quirks and personality traits, so people could look at their own habits and get started again, or tackle something they'd been afraid of.

Q: You talked about the writing process in a way that nobody ever had before.
A: Well, we editors see everything. It is like being a shrink; you have all these lives that you're ministering to.

To me, that work is endlessly fascinating. As an agent, my clients—the writers—never fail to amaze me, with the kind of crap they pull and with the leaps they make. I'm fascinated by everything they do. I applaud it and I support it.

Q: As a writer and an agent, you live on both sides of the fence at the same time.
A: The truth is that I don't. I live in my career ninety-nine per-

cent of the time and I live as a writer one percent of the time. I'm very engaged with other people's work, and I prefer it that way.

Q: Why don't you want to spend more time writing?
A: Maybe it's because I'm a publishing professional. I don't have any delusions about my talent or my abilities. There are things I would like to write, but that I'm not talented enough to write, or I don't have the discipline to write for hundreds and hundreds of hours, or thousands and thousands of pages.

I've written books that I was capable of writing, and I see how hard it is. I'm not interested in that struggle personally.

Q: Let's talk about the writers you work with. Have any of them responded to rejection in ways that have inspired you?
A: I have one writer whose novel I've been unable to sell for well over a year. She's adapting it as a screenplay, hoping that if she can pull that off, we can try again to sell it as a novel. *And* she's working on a new novel. She's not letting the defeat set her back. I'm very inspired by that. But for most people, if a novel doesn't sell, it takes a minimum of a year to get over it.

Q: If a year is the minimum, what's the maximum?
A: Some people stop forever. That's the worst tragedy of all. Unless you're just no good, and you really should be doing something else.

Q: Is rejection as hard on nonfiction writers as it is on novelists?
A: Nonfiction writers can write a proposal that won't sell and just write another. But because novelists have to write a whole novel in order to sell it, they get deeply involved with their characters and their books. Rejection for them is much worse.

Q: Have you ever had a writer who responded so poorly to rejection that you said, "I don't want to work with you anymore?"
A: No, because whatever their pain is, whatever reaction they

have, whatever acting out they might do, I feel for them. If I took the work on, I completely believe in it. I'm not going to back away.

I'm also suffering with them—although obviously it's a secondary pain. I try to motivate them, and inspire them to go forward, and not to take what happened as a declaration of their ability.

Some people really internalize the message—and it's crazy, because really lousy people get published and become bestsellers. It's all subjective, so there's no reason to question yourself. You have to find people who believe in you, and you have to keep trying.

Q: *Have you ever had an experience where someone's first novel didn't sell initially, but was published after they'd sold other novels?*
A: No. I have never had that happen. Usually a person whose first novel is published has three or four novels in the drawer that should just *stay* in the drawer. It's usually a bad idea to bring those old books out. I discourage it. I tell people, "Move beyond it. Show me your best work, your new work, the future." There are very few people who whose first book is a great novel.

Q: *A lot of people think your first published novel is the first novel you've ever written.*
A: Right. I mean, it's true for Philip Roth or Truman Capote, or people who clearly were geniuses at an early age, but for most people, not.

Q: *One of your authors, Carolyn Slaughter, published nine novels to acclaim, and then took a break to become a psychotherapist. Why did she stop writing?*
A: She was writing very dark, scary books, and she understood, at a certain point, that something was going on and she didn't know what it was. She finally went into treatment and became a therapist and mined her own past. After twelve years, she wrote a

memoir, and now she's writing novels again. Now her books are much less controlled by her demons, and more about what she really wants to talk about. She is one of my great inspirations.

Q: *So taming her demons didn't inhibit her creativity.*
A: On the contrary.

Q: *How do your authors tend to respond to reviews?*
A: People think writers are tough because they have a book and therefore they are successful and therefore they're impervious. People think that once you're published, you have it all. It isn't true. You *don't* have it all. You're just as fragile as ever. Nasty reviews can really take it out of you, and praise can warp you as well. So when people say, "I don't want to see my reviews," I think it comes from a place of very real self-knowledge.

Q: *Writers often don't remember positive reviews, only the negative ones.*
A: Almost every writer I know could quote, chapter and verse, the worst review or rejection letter they were ever given. That's how deep it gets into their marrow.

Q: *Rejecting writers has been a big part of your job as both an editor and an agent. How have you handled that?*
A: I have always used, as a rule of thumb, the advice our mothers give us, which is: "If you don't have anything nice to say, don't say anything at all."

Q: *Which means you use an innocuously worded form letter?*
A: I don't use a form letter. I have a few things I might say to someone who's work I'm passing on, and it *is* pretty generic.

Q: *The people on the receiving end of generic letters are often hurt and confused. Is there a solution to that?*
A: You have to educate yourself. The frustration tends to come

from people who haven't spent enough time and energy researching the market. Rejections from publishing people are meaningless. You simply have to be businesslike about how many people you approach. If your approach isn't working, change it. If you need help, hire somebody to help you.

A writer once said to me, "I sent fifty letters, and got fifty rejections." I said, "The letter probably sucked." She looked at me like, "*What?*" So I told her to send me the letter, and you know what? It was a disaster.

Q: Do writers come to agents with unrealistic expectations? Do they want you to give them feedback that they should be getting from other sources?
A: Yes. You can't look to publishing professionals to teach you how to prepare your manuscript. If you're getting rejected over and over again, join a writing workshop and see if the people in your group like the work. Take a class. Go to an MFA program. Hire a freelance editor. There are a lot of things you can do.

People always tell me, "I'd be grateful for detailed feedback." Yeah, I'm sure you would—but I have to pay the rent!

Q: Is there anything you would change about the rejection process if you could?
A: No. I think people have more chances of getting their books published than they do of getting their paintings into art galleries or getting their movies made. Publishing is still a very human process—you write it, I read it. It's one on one; there's nothing mystical about it. And it's fair. If you send your work to the wrong person, it's your fault.

I urge people to just be strong. Take your fragile writer self, put it on your computer and gather all the strength you have to get your work into the world.

Q: Do you have a theory about what makes some writers persevere when others don't?

A: I don't. I only know that perseverance is the only thing you can depend on. If you do not persevere, it probably will not happen. And most people do not persevere.

Q: You have a master's degree in poetry from Columbia University. Do you think getting an MFA really helps writers?
A: I think an MFA can be valuable when you're not published, to help you claim your identity as a writer. You may also find one or two people who become your ideal readers, and that is invaluable. And you see how your work affects people, and that also can be valuable.

You really have to look at what people *don't* like in order to learn anything. Whenever I teach a writing workshop, I always say, "Let's hear from the people who don't like it. They're the ones we're going to learn from."

That's when you find out how much you're invested in what you're doing. Are you going to change it? Are you going to dig in your heels? Learning to write is like breaking a horse. You have to learn how to get it under control. You have to make your writing say what you want it to say. You have to find out what it is you want to say.

So many young writers are clueless about what they actually want to say. Sometimes I'll tell a person what I think their book is about, and their eyes will fill up, because they didn't know.

Q: You've said that you'd rather see writers get inappropriately angry than have them turn that anger in on themselves.
A: Yes. I do think that internalizing rejection is going to kill you and make you stop. Getting feisty and angry is going to help you continue.

Q: You also said that any writer who is doing work of real interest is necessarily going out on a limb. But doesn't going out on a limb also increase your chances of being rejected?
A: No. Your chances of being rejected are high when you don't

write well. When you go out on a limb *and* you write well, people snap it up.

Q: You're giving me the feeling that there's actually an ordered publishing universe out there, where good is rewarded and bad is not.
A: Listen, when I have something that's A-plus-plus, it sells fast, for a lot of money.

Q: Is there a positive side to rejection?
A: Well, you know, most people who persevere will say, "I'm so glad I didn't ever publish that first book because I learned *x, y,* or *z,* or the timing was wrong." It's a huge process you've got to get perspective on.

Sometimes you write something and it's a huge failure. I am working on something right now, and I know it is going to be a failure—but I also know that I'm learning something about a kind of writing that I've never done before. And whatever I try next, I will have better developed writing muscles to possibly pull it off.

Writing is like working out at the gym or cooking—you have these disasters along the way. You have to pick up more skills and know-how about your craft—and that's what you're doing, as frustrating as it may be. When you turn a sentence better than you ever have, or you write a better story than before, it didn't just happen magically. You built up to that. And people who are the real thing just keep writing. They keep writing, because that's what they have to do.

ELINOR LIPMAN

PAUL SHOUL

"I try to remember that a review is one
person's opinion—and a cranky person's, at that."

*Elinor Lipman's humorous novels have been lifting readers' spirits
since 1987 when her first book,* Into Love and Out Again, *was published by Viking. Although early on some critics took her to task for
not being serious enough, today her ironic humor is widely appreciated. After the terrorist attacks of September 11, 2001, one editor
handed Lipman's books out "like aspirin," calling them "the literary equivalent of the Red Cross."*

*Lipman was born in Lowell, Massachusetts, in 1950. She
worked for nine years in public relations and corporate communications. Then, at age twenty-eight, she took her first continuing
education fiction class. Three years later, her first short story
appeared in* Yankee *magazine. Lipman's novels include* The Inn at
Lake Devine, Dearly Departed, Isabel's Bed, *and* The Pursuit of
Alice Thrift. *She has taught writing at Simmons, Hampshire, and
Smith colleges and received the 2001 New England Book Award for
a body of work. She lives in Northampton, Massachusetts.*

Q: What kind of business writing did you do before becoming a novelist?
A: I had various PR writing jobs, mostly for nonprofit agencies. In my first job out of college, I worked for New England Telephone doing their employee newspapers. I worked for WGBH, Boston's PBS station. And then I was a writer and editor for the Massachusetts Teachers Association.

Q: Were you rejected much during that phase of your career?
A: Well, in one of my jobs, I worked for an editor who we all considered to be moronic. Even with brilliant editors, one occasionally has to fight for one's sentences, so I suppose that was writing boot camp.

Also, I quit my job at the public TV station after three months, and I think I would have been fired if I had stayed. I couldn't do anything right. I think that taught me something, even if it's just maybe that you can rise up from the ashes. I like to say that when I'm speaking to groups of students. I like to let them know you can fail and then you can *not* fail; you can even succeed.

Q: One failure is not a predictor of what will happen next.
A: Yes, and in a sense it ties in with my career now. If there's a cranky review, I can say, "It's one person's opinion." When I had a boss I couldn't please it really *was* one person's opinion, because the people around me in the department were really supportive. They all wrote lovely recommendations for my next job. But I think there is an analog there of trying to please one unpleasable person.

Q: That experience taught you not to personalize rejection.
A: But it also brought out the worst in me! For example, when something really nice happens, like I have a piece published in the *New York Times*, what do I think of? I think, "I wonder if my old boss saw it."

Q: Has your former boss appeared anywhere as a character in a novel? Have you taken fictional revenge on him?

A: I did not evoke him in a novel, but I did in one of my short stories. I do think that fiction is a way to reward your friends and punish your enemies. I've taken revenge on someone who had given a very dear friend a very bad review in the *New York Times* by naming a sexual predator in *The Dearly Departed* after him.

Q: Do you find that once you write something like that, it gets it out of your system?

A: Apparently not! I still would like to see them with a dagger in their hearts. I'm afraid I have these little grudges.

Q: Tell me about how you sold your tenth short story, after the first nine were rejected.

A: When I sent the other nine stories out, I always would do research and send the story to a specific editor, by name, with a hapless little cover letter. I didn't have an MFA. I had nothing to brag about. What—I worked for the Massachusetts Teachers' Association?

Finally one day I just put a story called "Catering" in an envelope, with no cover letter and no editor's name. I just wrote, "Fiction Editor, *Yankee* Magazine" and put it in the mailbox. I was working in downtown Boston at the time. It's embarrassing to admit this, but I thought that if I used a particular mailbox and the story got rejected, I would try another one, because that mailbox became tainted. But this time, I just threw it in the mailbox thinking, "The hell with it."

There was no letter, no editor's name, and no lucky mailbox—and that was the first story that was accepted. It was my fortieth submission over the course of ten stories.

Q: What does that say about all the writing seminars that tell us to send a personal letter addressing the editor by name?

A: All it says is that my story was the right story for the right editor at the right magazine, and it didn't get lost because they had only one fiction editor.

The other ironic thing is that I used to put so much stock in my rejection letters. I would analyze the letter—if it had a name, if it was signed, if it was signed in ink rather than a stamped signature, if it said, "Please try us again" or "Thanks." And what I got from *Yankee* was a faded copy of a mimeographed acceptance letter. It said, "We hereby accept . . ." and then there was a blank and they had written in "Catering." I don't know what I thought would happen; I thought somebody would send flowers.

Q: Before the Yankee *acceptance, did you have a hard time continuing to send out stories?*
A: No, because I didn't expect a full-fledged acceptance. I recognized early on that some of my stories were not publishable, i.e. bad. I was looking for these little incremental improvements in rejections. Such as, as I said, a real signature.

The first thing that came that absolutely thrilled me as much as an acceptance would have was a handwritten index card that I found underneath my story, hidden behind a form rejection from the *Massachusetts Review.* And it said, "Please send more and I liked this story very much, and may I make the suggestion that you can bite off something a little meatier." I called home, I called my mother and father. And in fact, that story later got published.

I'm optimistic by nature. I knew I had to pay my dues, and I knew the legends of people who had three hundred rejections. So I can't say it came a little early because that sounds arrogant, but I was fully prepared to just keep doing this. When I got the acceptance from *Yankee,* I was thrilled.

Q: What about getting an agent and getting your first book published?
A: I didn't have difficulty in that area. Notice my voice just dropped because it's sort of embarrassing. I didn't pay my dues.

Q: But seriously, you had been writing fiction for how many years at that point?

A: I started writing fiction in 1978 and the story collection came out in 1987.

Q: So you did pay some dues.

A: I did. But when I look back, it seems sort of telescoped. I don't know whether I was patient, or whether I was getting enough encouragement from people who meant something to me, so that it kept me going.

But I'll tell you, my greatest pains have been suffered at the hands of magazine editors for freelance nonfiction articles. Maybe I had been spoiled by the editors in the publishing houses, who would buy a book based on one chapter, or even signed a two-book deal for something that didn't exist.

And then I would have to deal with a magazine editor, and I would write my little heart out for some essay, and it just wouldn't be "quite right." Those experiences have been the ones that have really felt like punches in the solar plexus.

Q: Even with a background of success in fiction, it still feels that bad?

A: Yes. A year ago a magazine solicited a piece through my agent. Before I sent it in, I first tried it out on my friends, one of whom is a Pulitzer Prize-winning nonfiction writer, another of whom is a bestselling author. They said, "Love it, love it."

Then I sent it to the editor and I didn't hear anything. That's the first insult. You don't hear anything and you don't hear anything. Then finally they sent me a proposed sort of recycled, rearranged article. I just said, "You know, I think this is not meant to be." Maybe I'm overly sensitive or maybe I'm spoiled, but really I grit my teeth over those.

Q: But you don't take them as an actual reflection on your writing.

A: No, actually. At this point, I fully blame the editor.

Q: That's healthy!
A: That's what I do! It would be one thing if I were writing in a vacuum. But my articles first go through my agent and my highly accomplished friends.

And then you're dealing with the editors' journalistic unscientific hunches about what people want to read in their magazine. It's not as though they read it and say, "I don't like it." It's, "Let me worry what the average reader will think of this." It's so annoying that I always vow, "That's it for magazine writing."

Q: So I'm not the only person who's made that promise! Now let's talk about reviews. Some critics have refused to take your writing seriously simply because it's humorous.
A: You know, I've gained some perspective on that over time. I don't feel damned or dismissed because of a label that some people have put on my writing. For one thing, I see what else is out there. I know that my publisher is very happy to be publishing me, and that humor is valued.

Also, I sometimes judge contests where I've had three hundred novels to read, and sometimes I don't find a glimmer of humor. You end up pouncing on the book that *does* offer some wryness, anything. And you can't help thinking, "Isn't it nice that I do something different?" I don't want to do what thousands of other people are trying to do.

Q: And humor is so badly needed—not only in writing, but in life!
A: Yes. I have to say, people who think that "serious" can't have any humor in it are not for me. They should go read someone else's books.

Q: When you get criticism, how do you deal with it?
A: The fairly healthy attitude I've developed, if someone writes something that seems to be dismissive, is that it's one person's opinion—and one cranky person's at that.

Q: You wrote back to a critic once, didn't you?
A: Yes. To my great regret. I did that twice, actually. The second one's a little known fact.

Q: What was the first one?
A: It was about my book of stories, *Into Love and Out Again*. It was one of my first reviews, in a now defunct publication on the West Coast. The main thing the reviewer said was that the book was charming, but that charm was the blight of the eighties. That was what I responded to. It seemed so pretentious.

Q: Do you remember what you wrote in reply?
A: I think I accused the reviewer of having no sense of humor. Essentially he was viewing the book through a sort of politically correct lens. He wrote, "Charm is the blight of the eighties, to wit Ronald Reagan." And of course I've never been able to see the charm of Ronald Reagan. And does that really belong in a book review?

Q: Why did you come to regret that letter?
A: I think experience tells you not to answer reviews, that it's undignified and unseemly. I never heard back from anyone at the publication. I'm sure it just struck them as "Churlish author responds."

Q: What about the second time you wrote to a critic?
A: I got a quite nice review in the *New York Times* for *Isabel's Bed* that began with a sort of topic sentence, a quote from Oscar Wilde: "All crime is vulgar, just as all vulgarity is crime."

Now, what the reviewer meant was that there was a crime in the book, and that the narrator was involved, and she was vulgar. But I thought he strained all the way through. He did end by saying that Harriet, the narrator, "chases her mischievous muse from vulgar premise to criminal end. Isabel's bed is serious entertainment." So it was a good review, but he tried so hard, it really bothered me. I wrote him a letter that said, "I found your review in the *Times* condescending and gratuitously insulting."

That was it. I felt much better, as if I had had some kind of pagan ceremony or exorcism where I had burned the review at sunrise on some beach. It was what I needed. That one I don't regret.

Q: *Did the* Times *reviewer respond to your letter?*
A: Yes. He wrote me this long, long letter about how much he liked the book. And my editor said, "If you answer him, I'll kill you."

Q: *I guess that's what editors are for! What advice have you given to writing students about coping with rejection?*
A: My very, very best advice, which I invoke a lot, came from Tracy Kidder. He was at an event before my first book came out, and I was expressing anxiety over the reviews. He said, very sweetly, "Could I presume to give you a little advice?" And he'd already won a Pulitzer Prize, for *The Soul of a New Machine*, and this was at least his third book, and I said, "Yes, please!"

He said, "There's the writing, and there's everything else. And everything else means sales, reviews, criticism, prizes." I just try to remember that—that there's the writing, and there's everything else, and you shouldn't confuse them. You shouldn't be judging your writing by those external things.

Another coping technique is this: When I start thinking about sales, and looking at attention that other people get—the people who just seem to be the anointed, the ones who are invited to *The New Yorker* panels, the ones who get full-page ads—I say to myself, "When you're thinking about those things, what you're really thinking about is envy and fame. What does that have to do with the writing, really?"

My job is not to micromanage my career in a way that might lead to a few more booksellers hand-selling my books. That's someone else's job. My job is to sit at the computer and write the books. The other things have to do with expectations of the book being out in the wider world, which is a real trap.

Q: If you don't judge your writing by sales, and prizes and things like that, how do *you judge your writing?*
A: By readers. That's another coping strategy—to remember the times that people have come up to me and told me stories that brought tears to my eyes.

A number of times people have said that they were sick or just had surgery. They say, "People gave me books on nutrition and visualization and trendy medical things, but someone gave me *Isabel's Bed* or *The Inn at Lake Devine* and I laughed." A woman came up to me at a reading and said her mother was dying. She was in a lot of pain. The daughter gave her *Isabel's Bed* and she could hear her laughing in the next room.

So when I start thinking about sales and reviews, I say to myself, "Remember that nice lady from Milwaukee? And if that has only happened five times, isn't that a lot?" These coping techniques work well when some shmuck was dismissive in a review. It doesn't even have to be in a review; it could be a curled lip or a glazed eye that you can't quite interpret at a reading.

Q: What happens when you're in a position to reject or judge the work of other writers? How do you handle that?
A: I'm very mindful of the fact that Flannery O'Connor said that her first stories were terrible, and that she would hate to be judged by them. So while you might be able to grade a particular paper and not like it, you shouldn't discourage the student. I always feel that the same amount of a person's heart and mind and soul go into a bad story as go into a good story, and that you always have to be kind.

BRET LOTT

RICK RHODES

"You cannot build the house of your life as a writer
and not include rejection as part of the foundation."

Bret Lott was enjoying a successful writing career when his then-publisher suddenly reneged on two books in a three-book contract. Stunned, Lott began the struggle to find a new publisher. In the meantime, he wrote about his trials and tribulations in "Mid-List Crisis: Why Write, Anyway?" for Poets & Writers Magazine. *Ironically, just when the article hit the newsstands, Oprah announced that Lott's novel* Jewel *was her latest pick. Suddenly publishers were in love with him again.*

Lott was born in Los Angeles in 1958. Among his published works are the novels The Man Who Owned Vermont, Reed's Beach, *and* The Hunt Club; *a memoir,* Fathers, Sons, and Brothers; *and two collections of short stories. He lives in Baton Rouge, Louisiana, where he is editor of* The Southern Review *and a faculty member in Louisiana State University's MFA program.*

Q: What made you decide to write that article for Poets & Writers?

A: It was originally a lecture I gave at Vermont College's low residency MFA program. As a writing teacher, you're always trying to teach craft, but students always have an eye on publication, publication, publication. I felt that I needed to tell that story, because students think that once you publish a single book, you're successful for the rest of your life. I wanted to tell them the truth about what you're up against, the parts people don't really talk about.

Q: That's the point of this book, too.
A: It's so easy for me to say this on the other side of it, but once you get through rejection, it's a lot more fun to write, man. It's fun!

In my lecture, I wanted to tell people, "You may see me as a success, but here's my story. Here's how I came to realize that it's about the characters, it's not about me. And one of the teachers at the lecture told me I ought to send it to *Poets & Writers*.

Q: Were you worried that Poets & Writers *would reject your piece on rejection?*
A: Actually no, because its audience had already heard it. Anything past that was cream.

Q: You talked about how your editor said, "The problem with your literary career is that you're white, male, and don't make good copy for People *magazine."*
A: My editor was on my side when she said that. She was making a rueful observation about the idiocy of the whole business of marketing. The funny thing is, since then I've been in *People* magazine three or four times.

Q: Was it a surprise when your publisher pulled out of a three-book deal after publishing only one of them?
A: It came out of the blue. My editor said, "You're gone," and two books that I had already written were tossed back to me. That was really a very difficult day. Even my agent was totally stunned.

I was in the middle of my career. I was in my mid-thirties and I had published five books, two with Viking and two with Simon and Schuster. And of course I started doubting myself. I decided I must be the one who was the problem, because they're big monolithic publishing houses, and they know more than I do. That's why it took me longer to write my next novel, because of the doubt I was experiencing.

Q: After your publisher gave you your books back, one of them was sold to a small press.
A: It was sold to Orchard Books, a children's press that decided to publish some adult things. They printed up a catalogue, and had the book bound and *everything*. Then they decided to quit.

That was a dreadful experience. It just blew me away. Meanwhile I was trying to write this other novel, *The Hunt Club*—and it sure took the wind out of my sails in terms of the confidence and authority that you need to write a novel.

Q: What kind of response did you get when you told these stories in the Poets & Writers *article?*
A: I got the sweetest mail I've ever got, from people I didn't even know. I was getting letters saying, "Thank you for telling the truth. Thank you for telling what really happens after you're published."

When Oprah called, there was a part of me that was kind of embarrassed, because here was this article on the newsstands, and everything I'd written about was kind of moot.

Q: Your credibility as a rejected writer was shot.
A: Really! I felt like, "Who's going to believe me now?" But a whole lot of things happened on that particular day that put everything into perspective.

My novel, *The Hunt Club*, had come out a year earlier, in 1998. Then I started writing a novel that I mentioned in the

Poets & Writers article—a story I wanted to write, even though I knew nobody in their right mind would ever publish it. But because *The Hunt Club* had done really well, the publisher asked me to write two sequels and gave me money for it. So I put away the book I had started, and I worked on a sequel to *The Hunt Club*. I was already over deadline for that novel on the day that Oprah called.

That day started out with my agent calling to tell me what I knew already—what I hoped she wasn't going to tell me—that the sequel just did not work. Then, at one-thirty that afternoon, after I had spent three hours talking to my agent, a fifty-one-year-old student of mine from Michigan was found in his dorm room. He had died from a brain aneurism. And he had my book, *Reed's Beach,* in his hand.

Q: What did you do? What did the school do?
A: Everything fell apart. We needed to have a meeting with the students and let them know what was going on. I was not holding together very well, but I volunteered to answer the phones during the meeting. I sat down in the office, and somebody called and asked for Bret Lott. "I'm calling from Chicago and my boss needs to speak to you, can you go on hold?" Then Oprah burst on the phone: "Bret, this is Oprah. We're going to have so much fun!"

The whole day had been about the pointlessness of the book business. Here I'd written a novel for money that had died; here's a guy who literally died, reading one of my books; and then Oprah called.

Q: You must have been in a state of shock. How did you cope?
A: I wrote that guy's name down on an index card and I put it in my pocket, and I kept it with me every day during the Oprah thing. Every day I would put my hand in my pocket and say, "This doesn't matter. Truly, we're going to all die. The question is, what are you going to do with your life right now?"

That's not to say that it wasn't great. It was a blast! And, iron-ically the people at Simon and Schuster who had given me the boot about six years before were now sending me flowers and champagne.

Meanwhile, my editor, my agent, and I decided, why publish another *Hunt Club*? The editor said," What else do you have?" And I said, "I just happen to have this novel about a woman whose husband has died." So the book that I had started writing when I knew nobody on planet Earth would care about it, is actually my next novel.

Q: It's so interesting that when you tried to write a big money-maker, it bombed.
A: Ugh! It was just bad! That book will never get published. I don't want it to get published. It just reeked of trying to reiterate something that had already been done.

Q: Let's go back to your early history as a writer. Before you sold your first novel, The Man Who Owned Vermont, *did you have many rejections?*
A: Yes. I sent short stories out, and I got rejected and rejected and rejected. For about fifty or sixty things that I published, I got more than nine hundred rejection slips. I bring them to class, and show them to my students. I say, "This is what it's about."

To me, rejection is the cornerstone of being a writer. You cannot build the house of your life as a writer and not include it as part of the foundation. If you don't acknowledge and accept rejection, your whole house is going to fall down. I know plenty of writers who don't deal with rejection well and who don't write. They believe rejection is a rejection of yourself and your talent, and it's just not so.

I make the students in my advanced writing classes submit a short story to a bona fide literary magazine. It's the final exam for the course. On the final day of class they bring a formatted manuscript, a cover letter, a self-addressed stamped envelope, and a stamped manila envelope. I seal it and I mail it for them. I tell them, "You fail this class if somebody publishes this story. I want you to get the rejection. Because if you don't get a thick skin, you're never, ever going to make it."

Q: You got twelve rejections before you sold your first novel. How did that feel?
A: It was very discouraging. I had just published a short story in an anthology called *Twenty Under Thirty,* so there were several editors who were interested in seeing it. I thought, "Oh, man, this is going to be easy!" Then each one of them turned it down—and for different reasons, too.

That was an education in itself. There was one rejection slip that said, "This is a hilarious romp of a first novel." Which it's not. And somebody else said, "Who's going to read a book about a cola salesman?" It took about nine months to get to Number 13, and by that time I'd pretty much given up.

I had not met my agent yet. I was going to go visit my in-laws in New Jersey, so I decided to go to the city and meet her. I took a train and walked down to Fourteenth Street and knocked on her door, thinking the whole time, "What am I going to talk about? Because all it's been is rejection, rejection, rejection."

She sat me down and said, "Viking called this morning and they want to buy the book." I just about flipped. I stood up and said, "Can I hug you?" After all the rejection, to have that delivered in my lap was a pretty wonderful thing. Then we went to lunch, and I told the waiter, "I just sold my first novel." He was a New Yorker, so he just gave me a shrug and said "Good for you," and walked away.

Q: In your Poets & Writers *article, you describe how a friend got you out of your funk by telling you to write for the fun of it.*
A: I remember that very vividly. And I thought, "That's exactly right. I've got to write because I want to write. I've got to write because I want to find out what happens to these characters."

Nothing miraculous happened, but I started inching closer and closer to the end of the novel. It was very much a return to the sense I had when writing my first novel when I was just a guy writing in the basement of an apartment townhouse, when nobody knew who I was and nobody cared what I was doing. It was very liberating—except I kept getting rejected.

The lowest point was when I got the phone call from my agent, saying "Bret, I think *The Hunt Club* might not get sold." My agent, who had been my number one fan, was losing faith in this book.

Q: One publishing company rejected The Hunt Club *because they didn't know how to market it. But isn't that what marketing people are supposed to figure out?*
A: That's exactly what I thought. I'm supposed to figure out my own marketing ploy? Isn't that your job? To me this is indicative of a kind of a cowardice that goes on in publishing. We think of editors as being superhuman intellects, but they're basically businesspeople. Instead of going out on a limb, the easy way is to take someone who's already pre-prepped and marketable and ready to go.

Q: What did your agent do after The Hunt Club *had been rejected by everyone?*
A: That's when she said, "Let's try it with a pen name." The first place she sent it was Random House. The editor called up and said, "Who is this guy? This is a great new voice." It was very funny. When they figured out who I was, they congratulated themselves: "We really do know a good book when we see it. We're so smart." Whereas if it had come with my name on it, I knew they would have said no.

Q: You've said that writer's block is an active choice not to take the joy of writing. What did you mean by that?
A: I don't believe in writer's block. Nobody is putting a gun to your head and tying your hands behind your back. You have a

pen in your hand, you have a computer monitor or a keyboard in front of you, and there is no reason you can't just sit and write. Writer's block is a self-inflicted head wound. You are the one who makes yourself write or doesn't make yourself write. There's *nobody* stopping you.

What I try to get my students to understand by getting that rejection slip is, you have to make accommodations to this. Otherwise you'll believe that an editor is right. An editor is a person who is breaking up with his wife, an editor is a person who has had a bad anchovy on a piece of pizza, an editor is somebody who has indigestion and seventeen manuscripts sitting on his desk, an editor is a guy who owes taxes. As soon as we start thinking about them as human beings, we realize that they're fallible.

Q: *Is there such a thing as a positive rejection?*
A: I believe there is good rejection that makes you a better writer.

The worst rejection slip I ever got was from Gordon Lish. I sent a story to *The Quarterly* and he scrawled across the rejection slip, "This is so derivative of Carver, it hurts." It was the only rejection I ever threw away. It cut me so deeply that I ripped it up.

But you know what? He was right. I think the reason I was so mad was *because* he was right. He saw me with my imitator's mask on. Carver is my hero, but I'm not Carver. That was a great rejection, because it throttled me to re-see the story through my own eyes, not Carver's. That particular rejection really made me a better writer. The question about any rejection is, What are you going to do about it? Are you going to learn from it or die because of it?

Q: *And then there are all the problems you have* after *a book is published.*
A: I got a sad, pleading letter just this week from a student of mine who just published her first book with a small press. She

said, "What's going on? The publicist is a ditz, they don't seem to be promoting it, they're not sending copies to the places where I give readings, and they're not getting enough people to review it."

I felt like sending her a little postcard that says, "Join the club, because that's what the club is about." Everybody thinks, "If I get a book published, my problems will be solved." It's not true. You just get a whole new set of problems.

Q: Do you read your reviews?
A: I would be lying if I said I didn't. A negative review is kind of depleting, but I want to know what's going on out there.

The Hunt Club got a huge review in the *New York Times Book Review* and it was absolutely nasty. The book had been doing really well, and it got tons of wonderful reviews. But then the *Times* came out with this savage review and I thought, "Omigosh, this is the end of the book." But *The Hunt Club* is now in about its fifteenth printing. That's proof that a bad review in the *Times* is not the end of the world.

Q: I think it's fabulous that you teach your students about rejection. Why don't more people do this?
A: I think there's a sense of wanting students not to focus on publication. It's like raising writers in a greenhouse and then expecting them to last the winter once they're outside. It's not helpful.

The fear is that you're going to taint the experience of art by creating it with your eye toward publication. That's not good, either, because you have to be inside the art to generate the art and not let the market be the dynamo or the engine behind it.

But my understanding of writing is that it's an act of communication. It's not a monologue. If I don't acknowledge that communicating a story means putting it out in a cold, anonymous world for someone else's acceptance, then I'm telling a lie about what writing is about.

If writing is not about trying to seek acceptance by someone else, then anything you write will be fine, because there's nobody else who needs to read it. And there's no reason to get better, no reason for clarity or precision, or emotional significance. That's simply keeping a journal. You're welcome to do that, but my definition of writing is an act of communication. And rejection is a part of it.

M. J. ROSE

MICHAEL BERGMANN

"The only reason writers survive rejection
is because they love writing so much
that they can't bear the idea of giving it up."

*M. J. Rose says rejection is the best thing that ever happened to her.
When her second agented novel,* Lip Service, *was turned down,
she took to the Internet and marketed herself so successfully that
her book was picked up by a book club and sold to a major publisher, while she was dubbed the poster girl of e-publishing by*
Time *magazine.*

*M. J. Rose was born in 1953 in New York City. She worked in
advertising before launching her career as an author. Rose's novels
include* In Fidelity, Flesh Tones, Sheet Music, *and* The Halo
Effect. *She is co-author, with Angela Adair-Hoy, of* How to Publish
and Promote Online *and is a contributor to* Writer's Digest, Poets
& Writers Magazine, O *magazine,* The Readerville Journal, *and*
Pages. *Rose lives in Connecticut.*

*Q: You began writing as a child. Did you ever feel rejected back
then?*

A: I'm dyslexic, but it wasn't diagnosed until I was thirteen, so I experienced a lot of failure in grade school. In fact, I was left back in seventh grade. That's a fairly huge rejection.

But it didn't have the effect on me one might imagine. My parents and teachers always believed in my intelligence and creativity and were baffled by my problems. Instead of punishing me, they always stressed what I was good at. I was always getting rejected and complimented at the same time, and that set a pattern for my entire life.

Q: *That was also good preparation for trying to make it in the publishing industry! When you started writing novels, how did you go about getting an agent?*
A: I didn't know anything about publishing, but in advertising I'd learned that there is always a faster way to get things done if you know who to ask. So I found someone who knew a lot about publishing, and discovered that the fastest way to get an agent was to hire a really excellent book doctor who had connections.

An ex-editor at Doubleday read my manuscript for a fee and accepted it. The next step was to finesse the book. Three months later, she sent the manuscript to an agent, who loved the book.

Q: *I like the way you just figured out what you needed to do and went out and did it.*
A: That's being a Jewish girl from New York in advertising. You can't make it if you're timid. I'm actually incredibly shy in social situations, but in business, I'm a different person.

Besides, I was in a hurry. I had a lot of books I wanted to write, and I was not going to spend five years trying to find an agent.

Q: *In the advertising business, spending money to get people to listen to you is not seen as a bad thing.*
A: Right. It's not the proper, white-glove approach of the literary

world. I think everything that happened, happened because I didn't start out in a traditional way. I was just oblivious to the rules of literary snobbism. And I'm glad I stayed oblivious—because I think I would have been intimidated and inhibited.

Q: *Tell me about how your first novel was originally rejected by the traditional publishing industry.*

A: My agent sent it to the twelve big publishing houses. Among them, two editors wanted to buy the book but... there was always a but. The rejection letters said, "I loved this book, but my marketing department doesn't see how it fits into the list."

My agent was told by editors that they felt that they could sell five thousand copies of that book, but they were looking for books that would sell twenty-five thousand copies.

Q: *How did you feel when you got those rejections?*

A: I felt sick. But my agent convinced me to write a second novel. That was *Lip Service.* Twelve houses, eleven rejections—all for the same reasons. My writing just didn't fit easily into a recognizable niche. We did get one offer, but it was rescinded before we went to contract because the marketing department felt the book would be too hard to sell.

I was inconsolable. Almost three years had passed from the day I hired the book doctor to the day the offer on *Lip Service* was rescinded. In fact, I became paralyzed.

During those same three years my marriage had been bad, and I had been holding off on doing anything about it until I knew what was going to happen with my novels. I had been hoping that if I sold one of them I could afford to support myself on my own without going back to advertising.

But there I was. Two finished novels. A fine agent. No deals. At that point, I'd been writing for six years and dealing with editorial rejection for three years. So instead of writing a third book right away, I left my husband and started on a nonfiction project.

Q: Could you read me one of the rejection letters you got for Lip Service?

A: Here's the worst one: "*Lip Service* is a well-written story with an intriguing premise . . . while Miss Shapiro's writing style is clear and straightforward, I felt the characters were not fleshed out enough to be truly appealing. Although this is a good first novel, I feel that I wouldn't be the right editor for the project."

Reading that out loud to you just gave me the chills. But that one didn't depress me nearly as much as the dozens of rave rejections I got—ones that ended with different variations of this: I loved this book, and please send me anything else from this author. But because this novel is both a mystery, and psychological and erotic, I'm not sure we'd know how to sell it.

Q: Those rejections are what got you involved in the Internet.

A: Yes. I had decided not to write a third novel but to write a nonfiction book that required a lot of research on the Internet. By 1997, after spending about two thousand hours on line, I'd come to realize that the Net was a new kind of communication vehicle—one that might lend itself to a new kind of marketing. So I had the idea to put *Lip Service* on the Internet and test my idea.

Q: Was your agent supportive of your self-publishing?

A: She wanted me to do the traditional thing, and just write another book, but when I couldn't, she understood. Her fear, back in 1997 and 1998, was that self-publishing was not the way to go. She didn't want me to get stigmatized as a desperate writer who wasn't good enough to get published.

Q: But you decided to do it anyway.

A: Yes. All I knew about self-publishing was that D.H. Lawrence, Anais Nin, James Joyce, and many other writers had published their own work for one reason or another. It all sounded romantic to me.

Everybody thought I was completely insane, but before long I was actually selling hundreds of copies of this downloadable book. The only glitch was that most people wanted to read a printed book, not an electronic one, so I was Xeroxing the book and selling it for twenty-five dollars. After a hundred of these, I thought, "This is really stupid. Why don't I just print the book?"

Q: Is it true that you had to sell your jewelry in order to publish Lip Service?

A: Yes. I sold all the jewelry that my ex-husband had given me to finance the publication of the book. This was a year before print-on-demand, so I had to do an actual print run. Then there were marketing expenses, including ads, banners, a cover, and a web site. The total cost to me was twenty thousand dollars.

In July of 1998 I put the book up for sale on the Internet, but nothing happened. I panicked. I only had a few months' worth of money left before I was going to have to go back to work full-time.

Then I had this epiphany: Here I'd spent my whole life in advertising, but I'd never bothered to put together an actual marketing plan for my own novel! So I spent a month working out a complete plan, and in November I began to implement it. By January, *Lip Service* had become the highest ranked small press book at Amazon.com and had been reviewed by over fifty Internet sites.

Q: How did you end up selling the book to a book club?

A: An editor at the Doubleday Direct book club heard the buzz that was building online and thought *Lip Service* sounded intriguing. In early 1999—three weeks before my money ran out—she wrote me an e-mail, asking for a copy of the book. At first, I thought it was a friend playing a mean joke.

Q: How did you figure out she was *for real?*

A: I called her. Two weeks later, she made an offer and I realized I'd just done something that had never been done. Nobody had ever used the Internet to generate buzz for a novel in order to get a publishing deal, and nobody had ever sold a self-published novel to the Doubleday Literary Guild—no less one that had begun its life as an e-book.

Within the week the news was written up in *New York Magazine, Newsweek,* and *Entertainment Weekly.* Meanwhile, my agent sent out the manuscript again. Within two weeks she held an auction, and Pocket Books bought the book.

I think I was incredibly lucky in being at exactly the right place at exactly the right time. I e-published a book before anyone knew what e-publishing was. A year later, Stephen King did it, and every news station wanted to find some little person who'd done it for a human-interest angle. I was the only little person who'd done it. So Stephen King got me a lot of press, and it was all very exciting.

Q: Was your agent surprised by what you accomplished?
A: Yes. I'll never forget when I called her to tell her the book club had bought the novel and did she think that might help selling it to a publishing house? She just started laughing. And she sold it within two weeks.

Q: Throughout this whole process, what kept you from giving up?
A: It was three things. Most important is that I couldn't imagine *not* writing. Then it was that my agent loved my novels and believed in me. And third, several of the editors had seriously wanted to buy my novels. So there were at least five people who really liked my stuff.

Q: Did it ever occur to you that maybe those five people didn't know what they were talking about?
A: No, I did not allow myself to go there, because it would have derailed me.

Q: What kinds of reviews did Lip Service *get?*
A: When I self-published it, it didn't get any print reviews. My first review was online, from January Magazine [www.january-magazine.com]. Their review opened up a lot of other Internet review sites for me.

But nobody reviewed it offline until it was published by Pocket Books. And then, people spent more time talking about how I'd self-published the book online and gotten picked up by New York than they did about the book.

Q: Were you bothered by that?
A: No. What had happened was so exciting and so huge! I went from being a self-published writer to sitting on the "Today" show in six months. It didn't even occur to me to be upset about reviews. There were too many things to be positive about.

When *Lip Service* was published by Pocket Books in the summer of 1999, many people saw self-publishing as a pathetic thing to do and assumed that if a book was self-published, it couldn't be good. But the world has changed. More than fifty self-published novels were picked up by New York publishing houses in 2002 and 2003.

Q: Besides, your readers take you seriously.
A: Yes. I pay more attention to fan mail than to reviews. Of course, we all want to get reviewed by the *New York Times*, and nothing would make me happier than getting the gray lady to give me a rave. But when I get upset about not being reviewed by some important paper, invariably within a day or two there's an email from a reader: "Your books are so special to me; you really reach a place in your writing that many authors don't. I feel like you must know me and that you are writing just for me." Letters like that put reviews in perspective.

Q: Is getting a bad book review as upsetting as getting a bad rejection letter?

A: Yes. I can get a dozen good ones but I will obsess about the one bad one. For hours.

Q: *And yet, you don't seem to be an insecure person.*
A: I'm just lucky in that my insecurity makes me work harder.

Q: *If you hadn't published anything, would you still be writing?*
A: I really believe that even if I could never be published again, even if there was no one who wanted to read my novels, I would still write—because the process makes me happy. Ultimately, the only reason writers survive rejection is because they love writing so much that they can't bear the idea of giving it up.

All you want before you are published is to get published. Then you get published and you realize it's all strangely anti-climactic. You get a pub date, and the book starts showing up in stores. Maybe you get readings and maybe twenty people show up. But there's nothing that competes with the writing process. Compared to that bliss, nothing happens when the book comes out.

Q: *The world goes on just as it did before.*
A: You've still got to make dinner and make the bed. And I think the longer you have been rejected, the worse that anticlimax hits. If you've been rejected for a long time, when you finally get published, you think, "Oh, it's all going to change now." It doesn't.

Q: *After all you've been through, do you recommend the self-publishing route to other writers?*
A: When I self-published in 1998, only a handful of writers were doing it. In 2002, over eighty thousand people self-published their books. The market is so flooded that I can only recommend it with caveats.

I believe you have to try to get an agent first. If you can't get an agent, I think the book must have problems, and the last thing you want to do is put a book out on the market that has problems. It's hard enough to get attention for a great book in this overcrowded marketplace.

If you get an agent and the agent can't sell the book because it will appeal to too small a market, *and* if you think there's a niche market that you that can reach effectively, by all means do it.

The African-American market for novels has a great network online of people who are more than willing to read self-published books if they come recommended, and so does the Latino market. Or if you've written something erotic, there's an equally strong Internet community for that. If you do your research on the Internet and you can find listservs and websites that reach over ten thousand people, then there's a real possibility.

Many authors have gone from self-publishing to big New York City publishing contracts. They were successful because they were able to find a niche market, get really good reviews online and make serious sales.

Q: What about people who can't get agents? Do they need to go back and rewrite their books?
A: I can't say for sure, but most of the time, yes. If a writer can't find an agent to bite, I'd suggest the writer take some classes, join a new writers group, go to some conferences and meet with editors, or hire a reputable book doctor.

Q: You've been called the patron saint of unpublished writers. What does that mean to you?
A: Nobody wanted to help me when I was unpublished, and everybody laughed and told me I was crazy. When I went on message boards to tell people what I was doing, a lot of people were horrendously negative and nasty.

I made the decision that if I ever *did* get published, I was not going to treat other authors like that. To that end I wrote two non-fiction books to offer to people who wanted advice. I also teach marketing classes for writers.

But more than that, I try to do whatever I can to empower authors, to help them understand that they have to become marketing partners with their publishers, and that they have to take their careers into their own hands.

Q: Do you ever get dissed by anyone because of your self-publishing origins?
A: I used to. Now, with several novels published traditionally, my self-publishing beginnings are rarely mentioned anymore.

But I'll never forget going into a local bookstore to ask if they would stock a couple of copies of *Lip Service*. The owner said, "I wouldn't even *look* at a self-published book." I never tried to get into another bookstore. I'd been rejected enough; I didn't need people who owned bookstores rejecting me, too.

Q: Do you think your background in advertising made it easier for you to see publishing more objectively?
A: Yes. Authors are typically not businesspeople. Not that I blame them. But I personally think that it's important for every writer to learn about the publishing business.

Q: That way, when you get the inevitable rejections, you're not going to be shocked.
A: If you know that out of one hundred and fifty thousand manuscripts submitted a year, only five hundred are sold, you won't feel so bad when you get rejected. You'll know what your odds are.

Q: Your rejections forced you to reevaluate your writing and your life.
A: I'm probably the only writer in the world who is actually glad they were rejected. Had *Lip Service* been sold to a publisher back in 1996 or 1997, I would have become just another new novelist

with another nice novel. I would never have become the first person to have done anything.

I may never write a Pulitzer Prize-winning novel, but I will go down in history as the first novelist to use the Internet to publish a book successfully. I never would have done that if I hadn't been rejected. From that point of view, rejection is the best thing that happened to me.

ESMERALDA SANTIAGO

FRANK CANTOR

"I write the best book I can and hope for the best.
Like when you give birth to a child and
hope that he doesn't grow up to be a serial killer."

*Long before she had to face rejection from editors or critics,
Esmeralda Santiago had to deal with the trials of learning a new
language and culture when she moved to Brooklyn from Puerto Rico
at the age of thirteen. Santiago overcame poverty and prejudice to
graduate from New York City's Performing Arts High School and
from Radcliffe College. She is the author of three memoirs,* When I
Was Puerto Rican, Almost a Woman, *and* The Turkish Lover.
Santiago's other books include a novel, America's Dream, *and with
Joie Davidow, two essay anthologies. Her work has won numerous
awards, including the American Library Association's Alex Award.
Santiago is also a lecturer, actor, dancer, activist, and filmmaker.
She lives in Westchester County, New York.*

Q: How did you begin your career?
A: I worked for many years as a bilingual secretary, and part of
my job was writing my boss's letters. Many people told me I

wrote good letters, but I never valued my ability to write. After I graduated from college, I wrote proposals for nonprofit organizations, and people said they enjoyed reading them—which is pretty amazing if you've ever read proposals! So I began to believe that maybe there was something to my writing.

I took an extension course through Radcliffe with a poet, and he encouraged me to try to publish. Then I moved to New York to get a master's degree in writing. In May, *Radcliffe Quarterly* published one of my essays. That summer, Addison-Wesley called me, and one month later, they sent me a book contract.

I had just started graduate school and didn't know what it meant to get a contract. I didn't realize it meant they would be paying me. I started school at Sarah Lawrence and I asked my advisor, "What do I do about this book contract?" She said, "You take it!" And that's how it started.

Q: Since you've never been rejected, does that mean you never worry about rejection?
A: I think you always worry and think about it. It's the nature of the business that whatever you write, somebody has to pass on it. When I send something to an editor, there's a chance that she won't want the book or that it wasn't what they wanted or that somebody else came out with a book just like mine. A million things could be grounds for that book never seeing the light of day. I know writers who have received contracts and been paid, and the books were *still* not published.

I do worry about rejection when I send the manuscript off. But my attitude is, I write the best book I can and hope for the best. Like when you give birth to a child and hope that he or she doesn't grow up to be a serial killer.

Q: Were you surprised that your first book, When I Was Puerto Rican, *generated so much interest?*
A: It was a total surprise. I thought eleven copies of the book would be sold—one to each of my siblings, and the one I would

have to buy for my mother. I never thought anybody else would have any interest in it. No one was more surprised than me that the book would have so many readers, or that it would be adopted by school systems as part of their curriculum.

I was also surprised because I didn't think of myself as a writer. I went to a lecture given by Jamaica Kincaid, and she said that if she couldn't write, she would die. I knew that if I didn't write, I could always be a secretary. Writing is one of the things I do. My sense of who I am is not built up around my writing.

Q: So if your books weren't published, you wouldn't mind?
A: I would be disappointed, I would not be as happy as I am, but I don't think I'd die. There are so many other things in life!

Q: In other words, it's important to have a life.
A: Any time you put all your eggs in one basket, you're bound to be disappointed. First you want to get a book published, then you dream of being on the bestseller list, then you think, if only they made a film about your book. But maybe that's not really what makes you happy. Maybe what makes you happy is just setting all those goals.

So I try to keep my perspective. I try to have a healthy relationship to my writing and my writing life. This is what I *do*, not who I am and what I am. I would be a really boring person if that was all there was to me.

Q: Did anyone in your family reject you because of anything you wrote about them in When I Was Puerto Rican?
A: When the book was close to getting published, I was quite worried about that. I thought, "People are going to throw tomatoes at me." But my family has been really supportive and encouraging. They love the book and they thank me for writing it.

Q: Did you show the book to your family before it was printed?
A: No. I sent them the first hard covers that came in.

Q: That was brave of you!
A: What choice did I have? I wouldn't have changed anything. Memoir is a very personal art form, and in order for it to be effective it *has* to be personal. I wrote the best book I could have written. I was writing about what I remembered, not what happened, and I was very clear about that.

Q: What do your family members like about your books?
A: I think they like the fact that I'm doing something that I love. They also knew that I wasn't going to break their trust, and that they didn't have to call me and say, "Please don't write about x, y or z." They expected that I would know what to leave out of the book.

The other reason is because they, just like me, did not find a lot of reading material that discussed the experiences we had. They were just as hungry for it as I was, and as so many of my readers were. Their reactions were the same as the reactions that I get on my web site from people who have come to my books for the first time: "At last somebody is writing something that is a reflection of my life. At last I am not alone in this struggle."

In one sense, my family really came to the book as readers, and not as protagonists in the story. And finally, we all feel that whatever I have written is about the way it *was*. Their lives are different now. They are really proud of who they have become, and they're not at all defensive. They're my biggest fans.

Q: Some essayists and memoir writers wonder if they have the right to write about their families.
A: I think most beginning memoir writers worry too much about that. Because ultimately, if you write a book that's fair and that's truthful, your loved ones are not going to get too upset. If you write lies, then they have every right to do that.

You have to do your best to be honest and truthful, and let them know that this is what you're doing: "I'm writing *my* mem-

oir and not *yours.* You happen to have been in some of the events
that I'm writing about, but it's not about you."

*Q: There was one brother who was upset that you left something
out...*
A: My brother Hector had a lizard circus when he was a kid. He
trained them to jump little hoops and stuff like that, and he was
very upset that I didn't mention this accomplishment!

Most of the time, what people are upset about is not necessarily what you *think* they're going to be upset about. They're
frequently upset that you didn't put in their moments of glory—
and sometimes those moments of glory, you don't know what
they were.

Q: Do readers ever give you negative feedback?
A: Readers are very honest and open. They come up and tell me
what they don't like, and they have no qualms about saying, "I
liked your first book better and I don't like the second book
because..." They will tell you in a way that even a critic won't.

Q: How do you respond?
A: I thank them for their opinion, and for at least being passionate enough about my work to have an opinion. The reader I
worry about is the one that throws the book across the room and
never reads it. The one who has something to say about it, is a
good reader. I'm grateful for these readers, even if they criticize
me.

Q: Do you ever receive criticisms that really bother you?
A: I don't read my reviews, because I find they're really counter-
productive. I would only get depressed. So I don't really pay
much attention to that. I listen to my editor, my agent, and my
writers' group.

Every writer has strengths and weaknesses. There are some
people who are much better at plotting out a book than at writ-

ing eloquent poetic descriptions. Well, there are some readers who don't want to bother with eloquent poetic descriptions. They just want to get through the story.

Criticism and reviews are subjective, and they're not necessarily representative of the people who love the kind of writing that you do. So I really, truly do not read them.

Q: Has anyone ever given you nasty criticism to your face?
A: The only face-to-face encounter I ever had was with a Puerto Rican professor at CUNY [City University of New York]. He was a friend of a friend, and we all had a lovely lunch, and just as he was leaving he said to me, "I would never teach your book in one of my classes. It's just another book about a poor, single, Puerto Rican mother on welfare. It's just another stereotype of Puerto Ricans."

My response was, I wish that had *not* been my life. I wish I had been raised in a life of privilege. But this is a memoir; this is reality.

There is no sense in arguing or trying to convince certain people. For all I know, that professor is still not teaching my book. But it doesn't matter to me. It's so much less important to me than the fact that the book was written. It was a very hard thing to do, and I take pride in having done it.

Criticism has to be specific and meaningful for me to take it to heart. That was just stupid.

Q: What's an example of criticism that has *been meaningful?*
A: I just brought a short story to my writers' group. They made suggestions that the ending would be better if a certain character did something other than what she does at the end. The ending I had was not focused. So they said, "What if she did this, instead of doing that?"

It was the perfect suggestion. I probably would have come to that after twenty drafts of the story. But instead I came to it after two drafts. They gave me a suggestions I could use that actually helped me to become a better writer.

Q: You seem to be very secure both as a person and as a writer.
A: What has given me a sense of security is that I have survived so many other types of humiliations.

Q: Such as?
A: Such as being a non-English speaker in an English-speaking world. As a child, going with my mother to the welfare office to translate for her. At college, always being the darkest-skinned person in the room. At Harvard, having everyone think that the only reason I was there was because of affirmative action. All these things are a part of my experience.

It takes a lot to offend me at this stage in my life. Now that I have developed my own sense of who I am, I place very little stress on what other people think. I am my own harshest critic in terms of my writing and in terms of the way I live my life. And I have arrived at a point in my life that if I am okay with all my decisions and choices, what business is it of anybody else's? That's very free-ing. Of course there are moments of insecurity, and moments when I'm not really sure that I've done my best, but I don't let them paralyze me. I use them as an opportunity to get better.

Q: In other words, the adversity you've faced has made you stronger?
A: I think adversity either makes you stronger or completely destroys you. I don't know what the trick is to make it go one way or the other, but in my case, the tougher things were, the more I used them as opportunities to go forward. I didn't let them paralyze me. It was almost a revenge, actually. When some-one said to me, "No, you can't do that," I was determined to show that yes, I could.

That happened to me a lot, starting in my very early life. When my mom started to leave the house to go to work, that was a really tough time for us. Kids would make fun of us, and their mothers would whisper behind my mother's back—but I never wavered in my belief that they were wrong and we were right.

Q: Why not?
A: Even though we grew up with so much less than other people, we were always confident of the total, unconditional acceptance that our parents had for us. I think when you grow up
feeling loved, that goes a long, long way to get through adversity.
This person who is being rude or mean to you doesn't love
you—but it doesn't matter, because your mom loves you, and
your dad loves you, and your sisters and brothers love you. And
that, ultimately, is much more important that whatever any
stranger might think. I just would never do *anything* to disappoint my sisters and brothers, but if I disappoint Michiko
Kakutani or some other critic, I don't care.

*Q: I was intrigued to learn that your dad was a writer who always
carried a notebook around with him.*
A: My dad has been a poet and an avid reader of the poets of
Puerto Rico since he was a very young man. He was an itinerant
handyman, a jack-of-all-trades. I've seen him, when he was
working on a wall or floor, stop whatever he was doing and sit
under a tree and write a poem in his notebook. But he never
wrote with the intention of being published. Poetry for him is
just an expression of himself, and the idea of publishing was not
a part of that.

Q: Did your father's poetry influence your becoming a writer?
A: I think maybe some of that rubbed off on me, because I have
a very artisanal approach to writing. It's what I do, and I don't
need to have perfect silence and candles burning and the room
painted purple—none of that. The fact that writing was valued
in our household definitely had an influence. I didn't think of
writing as something weird. If you were washing the dishes and
all of a sudden you were inspired, you just went and wrote in
your notebook. It wasn't something precious; it was a part of
who you were. Inspiration could strike at any moment, and you
just followed it because it was so fleeting.

Q: *Do you have any advice for other writers on how to deal with rejection?*

A: I think you are just going to have to grow up about it. I know it's hard to do. But it's part of developing as an artist. You have to get to the point where you're confident enough in your work to see that it's not *you* who's being rejected; it's something in your work that is not connecting with the other person. Then you have to decide if you think the criticism is valid, or if you just have to say, "I respect the integrity of this work," and go on to the next project.

It's a big, big struggle for an artist to get to that point. Some people never get there. But whether you're going to be happy with your art hinges upon whether you're able to do that.

BOB SHACOCHIS

"Writing well is the best revenge."

Bob Shacochis describes himself as unstoppable in the face of rejection—and he's had plenty of it. In his youth his parents tried to discourage him from becoming a writer. Early in his career, several literary agents advised him to stop writing short stories. Instead he completed the National Book Award-winning collection Easy In The Islands. *His second short story collection,* The Next New World, *was awarded the Prix de Rome by the American Academy and Institute of Arts and Letters, and he has also received a James Michener Fellowship and a grant from the National Endowment for the Arts.*

Shacochis is also the author of the novel Swimming in the Volcano, *a finalist for the National Book Award; and nonfiction books* The Immaculate Invasion *and* Domesticity: A Gastronomic Interpretation of Love. *He is editor of* Literary Trips: Following in the Footsteps of Fame, *and he writes regularly for* Gentleman's Quarterly, Outside, *and* Harper's. *Shacochis was*

born in 1951 in West Pittston, Pennsylvania, and lives in
Tallahassee, Florida.

Q: What can you tell me about the role of rejection in your career?
A: Well, I've been enormously lucky. Any writer who has published and who doesn't admit that probably has a narcissism
problem.

Rejection is something you have to prompt a writer to think
about, unless they obsess on rejection, which I doubt that they
do. At least in my instance, it's not something I think about a lot.

Q: Well, that's good!
A: There's a good reason for that. You simply can't dwell on it.
There has to be something unstoppable in your nature if you're
going to persevere through the natural and sometimes unnatu-
ral rejections that you're going to encounter from the day you
decide to commit yourself to a writing life.

*Q: Are you born with that unstoppableness or is it something that
has to be cultivated?*
A: I don't know if you can cultivate obsessiveness or not.

Q: Do writers have to be obsessed?
A: You absolutely do. I have topics I want to write about stacked
up in my life like airplanes over La Guardia waiting for landing.
They're all obsessions, and they all seem to be there from the
original day of adult consciousness engaging with the world.
Out of that engagement, obsessions started popping up all over.

Q: It would probably be harder to figure out how to get away *from
your obsessions than to find more of them.*
A: Yeah. Give me five lifetimes to actually process all those projects I would love to get working on!

Q: When did you realize that you had this unstoppable quality?

A: When people began to tell me, no. It was a childhood dynamic. When my parents said yes, I said no. When they said black, I said white. When the government told me one thing, I said, No way. That unstoppable quality seems to be a direct result of resisting the received wisdom of parents, authorities, whatever.

And I don't think I was just being frivolous. I clearly remember being told that reality was one thing, and disagreeing with that. When people, especially my parents, tried to keep me from being a writer, it quickly evolved into that "I'll show you" type of unstoppableness that you get when you have to prove something to somebody.

Q: So your first rejection as a writer was from your parents.
A: Yeah. They thought it was a foolish gamble. They couldn't perceive the shape of the lifestyle. You don't go to an office, you don't get a paycheck, what the hell is it you do? It didn't make any sense to them.

I suppose, in my most rosy interpretation of all this, they were simply trying to protect me from failure. But, as anybody knows who pursues their dreams and achieves their dreams, you don't try to de-dream somebody. That's castrating the dog. You don't castrate the dreams out of your children.

Q: Are your parents proud of your writing success now?
A: Now, certainly, they see it as something they can brag about. But they've also had to take hits for it. For instance, when my book, *Immaculate Invasion,* came out, it was reviewed on the front page of the *Washington Post Book World.* There was a book review by a writer I really despised. It was malicious and spiteful, and he called me a coward. Meanwhile, my parents are well-known people in the Washington area. So they've had to live with some of the glory and the fall-out of my career. But early on, it was something that they basically didn't express much interest in.

Q: Your first book, Easy in the Islands, *won a National Book Award. Did you have a hard time getting it published?*
A: My agent is very protective of her writers. In our conversations over the years, she has mentioned how hard it was to get that book published, but she never let on at the time.

Q: Did you have a hard time finding an agent?
A: I didn't, and here's why. I was a student at the Iowa Writers' Workshop, and Iowa has terrific resources for its young aspiring writers. In my first year there, I signed up to have conferences with four or five agents. They all said "I love your short work, I think you're really good, and when you grow up and write a novel, get back in touch with me." This was in the 1980s, the boom of the short story renaissance, and I thought they were ridiculously bad businesspeople. It made more sense to me that, if they thought I was a capable writer and they really wanted to make a splash out of a novel, what better approach could you have than to build a reputation through the short stories?

Finally I met an agent who was of the same mind about developing a reputation through the stories in order to make the job of selling the novel easier. And that's exactly what happened.

Q: How do you react to really nasty criticisms?
A: With a great black sightless fire of hatred. I'll tell you how I reacted to my first bad review, and it was a doozie. It was on my first book, and it was the first time I'd been reviewed in the *New York Times Book Review*. The review was by a radical feminist poet, and the headline was "Free, White and Hairy-Chested." If I had been a Jewish girl from Asbury Park, New Jersey, would the headline have been, "Free, Ashkenazi and Big Breasted?"

Q: How can you defend yourself against that?
A: Well I didn't, but John Irving did. He wrote a four-page, single-spaced, typewritten diatribe to the editor of the book review

section saying, How dare you do this to young writers? I didn't even know about it until afterwards.

Q: *What was the main criticism of the book?*
A: That the women were treated like dirt underfoot. I still have to scratch my head and take deep breaths on that one, because several stories in the book are about women coming into their own strength and giving comeuppance to the jerks in their life.

With that kind of review, it's just torturous. You think, "My God, how could I be so misinterpreted? Did I really screw up that bad? Am I that bad of a writer that the trajectory into strength of my female characters is not clear?" And then you realize that you were screwed by somebody with an agenda.

Q: *That kind of review can tap into a writer's own underlying self-doubt.*
A: I have the reverse reaction to that. When somebody tells me I can't do something, or I did something poorly, or I am somehow not capable or not worthy, my self-doubt is totally obscured by my anger.

Again it goes back to that notion of unstoppableness. I want to prove them wrong. My confidence really is born out of that urge. Living well isn't the best revenge; writing well is the best revenge! The best revenge is being something they tell me I can't be, and achieving something they tell me I can't achieve.

In the quiet of my own life and my self-evaluation, I have great self-doubt. I doubt my ability to write the books I want to write, I doubt that I'll be allowed to participate in the literary village at the level of engagement I want, I doubt my ability to participate in the level of national discourse that I want to participate in. I will always have self-doubt about those things. The only time I have some relief from the self-doubt is when somebody pisses me off. That's when my confidence is assured.

Q: Winning the National Book Award doesn't provide any relief from self-doubt?
A: God, no! I don't think there's any relief anywhere all along the line. I just have another higher, and yet denser, level of pressure.

If you're not publishing at all, and then you're published in a literary magazine, you certainly can raise a glass of champagne and toast your success for a day, but you still have to keep publishing. And as you move up the ladder of visibility into the general interest magazines, you're competing for space with all the people who were your role models and heroes when you were just a minnow. And if you wrote a good book today, does that mean you're going to write one tomorrow?

Any creative activity, whether it's writing or acting or painting, the better you come at it, the more you increase your chances for national and international humiliation.

Q: But given all that, you still don't seem to be a miserable person.
A: I'm an optimist. I love life and I love people. These are the real tools for moving ahead in your life and doing what you want to do.

Only *I* can make myself miserable. Other people can make me feel bad, but they can't make me miserable.

Q: You make anger sound like something positive. Do you consider yourself an angry person?
A: It's really more passion than anything. There's an intensity to my personality that people don't often find comfortable. When it's really cooking. I can't have a mellow-voiced conversation about important things; I get passionate about them.

Q: You need that passion to keep you going, no?
A: Yes, but you also need some diplomatic skills to make the business side of your writing *not* a disaster.

Q: Speaking of, you were once a fiction editor at the Missouri Review. *Is it true that your main job was saying no?*
A: That's mostly what a fiction editor does. The ratio of *nos* to *yeses* is extreme. Even if you wanted to say yes a lot more, the physical format of publication isn't going to allow you to.

We published only one story a month. And most of the magazines that still publish fiction can only publish one a month, so that's just twelve writers a year. You're saying no thousands of times, and there's no alternative to that except to have more magazines.

Q: Does that mean the slush pile really is a hopeless place?
A: I did an interview for the *Missouri Review* with Chip McGrath, who was one of the six fiction editors at *The New Yorker* in the seventies and eighties. They get three to four hundred stories a week, and I asked him how often a story comes out of the slush pile. He said maybe once or twice year.

But what *does* come out the slush pile is a writer. You see a particular writer who shows great potential, and you start a dialogue with that writer. "I really admire what you're doing, and I would like to encourage you to keep sending new stories." Usually when you get that far toward intriguing an editor, if you persevere, it's going to pay off.

I wrote letters to the writers that I wanted to see in the *Missouri Review.* One of them was Jay McInerny, who had not yet published *Bright Lights, Big City.* One was a very young writer from Columbia [University] who was just beginning to publish her first stories: Mona Simpson. I know that I didn't send them form rejections.

Q: Because you recognized the quality of their work.
A: Yes. I remember quite distinctly, sending a letter to Mona, having a correspondence with Jay and a few other writers.

Q: Did you learn anything from your experience as an editor that helped you as a writer?

A: I learned that wherever you're mailing work to, a lot of other people are mailing their work there, too. And the people who are trying to process it are very overextended. They're trying to deal with the slush pile with respect and engagement and a sense of integrity, instead of becoming cynical and exhausted. They are working very hard to create a good magazine or journal.

Also, I learned that really good writing, like any cream, rises to the top.

Q: *Do you really believe that?*
A: Yes. I certainly believe it. Somebody's got to prove to me that the cream *doesn't* rise to the top. What we *can* disagree on is how long it takes. Sometimes it can take forever. Sometimes it's posthumous. But it rises.

You just don't hear too many stories about John Kennedy Tooles—of a person who's been rejected all his life being discovered when the executor of their will passes the manuscript on to an editor.

Q: *Why doesn't that happen more often?*
A: Because I don't think that the system we have for discovering and publishing writers in America doesn't work. I think it works. Even for the best, most successful writers, it's a frustration to deal with the system—but it works.

Q: *I think one of the biggest frustrations for people who are just starting out is the slowness of it.*
A: Well, you know, I don't have any sympathy for editors in this respect. I know they're overworked, but I'm a writer, not an editor. I don't hesitate to tell my students in writing programs, "All's fair in love and war in getting published," and, "Do multiple submissions."

My God—to send something to *Paris Review* and wait a year to get a rejection? The hell with that! Do multiple submissions, and if someone takes it, have enough integrity to call everybody else up and withdraw it. You don't have to say *why* you're withdrawing it. Say you need to withdraw it, and you'll be sending them something else. But you can't wait and wait and wait. It's ridiculous!

Q: What else do you tell your students about dealing with all the frustrations?
A: Be a professional. Once you have established the fact that you're professional and you're committed and you're going to persevere, no matter what, then write for yourself. Because you're never going to make anybody happy writing for them. Artists have to focus on their art, and sooner or later maybe lightning will strike. Talent just gets you into the game, and then luck makes you win that game.

Q: A lot of your fiction is set in the Caribbean. Have you ever been criticized for appropriating someone else's culture?
A: *Harper's* ran a piece of mine a while ago, called "The Enemies of the Imagination," and it was totally about this issue. [The article appeared in November 1995.] The article is part of a longer piece that was published in the journal, *Points of Contact*. It was a presentation I gave at a conference on cross-cultural writing at the University of Nevada, where Ana Castillo looked across the table at me and said, "I don't want to be on a panel with a white guy."

The fact is that anybody who is going to censor the imagination is also going to be guilty of censoring the ability to empathize and the ability to have compassion. To take these things away from humanity would be a great crime, and to take away the ability of a writer to imagine his or her way into the other's life would be a great cultural crime.

Q: Boy, you're really getting it from every side for being a white guy!
A: I used to cry about it a lot, but now I just think it's so fatu-

ous. I also think the argument has moved on, and the people who cling to it are so marginalized, and everybody is tired of listening to them whine. This is an issue we got through in the nineties, and it has resulted in a great explosion of voices on the American artistic scene, and so: Problem solved! More or less.

I think there are enough people in all communities and races and ethnic groups today who understand that this argument is really thin, and will get thinner. Because real artists do not want to be limited by any political agenda.

Q: And where do you draw the line? Do you then have to say that a woman can't write a character with a male's point of view?
A: It's a big question, and it goes far beyond literature, to how we really learn to live together—and that is through imagining each other's lives. It is the quintessential act of coexistence.

Q: And it also goes to the heart of what any art is all about.
A: Right. Because *everybody* is the other. With that political agenda toward art, the very first thing that would have to go is any historical writing. Because, hey, you weren't there—how could you know? And that would be a great loss.

Q: When you first got that kind of criticism, though, how did it feel?
A: It felt just fine, because I had always had friends in the communities that I was writing about. I was showing my work to them to make sure there wasn't something I was overlooking—for instance, my own arrogance. It was important to get the nod from them before I had courage to be published. Once I had it, once I understood that *they* understood that I was writing in good faith about their lives, then it didn't matter what anyone said to me in public.

I remember Janet Burroway once said to me that I was condescending to class and race because I put dialogue into dialect, into Caribbean patois. I told her it would be condescending *not* to do that. That's *their* voice.

Q: It would be like dressing someone up in a suit and tie...
A: ... so you can take them to the club, and they won't embarrass you with their bad language. It's not bad language at all, it's very beautiful language. And it's *theirs*.

Q: Otherwise you're putting a moral judgment on that language.
A: It's a class judgment, really. And ultimately that class judgment is based on a moral value system that I just could never agree with.

Q: Speaking of systems you couldn't agree with—you had a rocky time in journalism school, where your teachers considered your work to be pretentious.
A: Well, that was fine with me, because they all came from second-rate newspapers, and they were interested in training the infantrymen of journalism to write "who, what, when, where" stories in the most simplistic language. That wasn't the thing that attracted me to journalism at that time in my life. Those were the days when great magazines were publishing Gay Talese and Hunter Thomson and Tom Wolfe and all this fabulous New Journalism. That's what I was engaged in as a journalism student.

What those teachers did, which is so very important, is they gave me an absolute respect for accuracy. They also gave me an absolute disrespect for their own rejection of language. In one feature-writing class, they asked me to write a seven hundred-word piece about the most beautiful lawn contest in the ghetto. I went to the ghetto in Columbia, Missouri, and I looked around, and I wrote a twelve-thousand word piece on the inanity of the most beautiful lawn contest in the ghetto and what the hell's a ghetto doing in Columbia, Missouri, in the first place? They flunked me.

Talking about unstoppableness, too, when I got out of the Peace Corps in 1976, I thought, Why not roll the dice on the whole pot here and get into a writing program and go towards the full bloom of the dream of writing fiction and literary non-fiction? And so I applied to all the graduate writing programs in the country. But they all rejected me.

Q: Were you shocked?
A: I certainly was disappointed. I probably wasn't shocked because I didn't believe in my writing enough at that point. But my literary godfather, William Peden, who started the under-graduate writing program at the University of Missouri, gave me a teaching fellowship, and I got an M.A. in literature and worked on a newspaper for a year. Then I reapplied and got into Iowa, which had initially rejected me.

Q: Did you have the sense the second time around that you were really ready to be accepted?
A: Well, I had that sense the first time around—but that didn't fit anybody else's reality! The second time around, I didn't know if it could happen. When I sit down to write, I *still* don't know if it can happen. Every morning, when I sit down to write, the question for the day is, "Am I a writer?" So far the answer has been yes, but I don't have any solid certain feeling that tomorrow it's going to be yes.

Q: So what keeps you going?
A: Writing is a lifestyle that I can't walk away from. I could be a full-time journalist or a full-time academic, but neither of those professional milieus, even though they have some of the free-dom and space that the writing life has, are survivable to a per-sonality like mine. I'm a bad team player. "Does not play well with others." Plays well enough with other people, but institu-tionally—never!

I've learned that perseverance is much more important than

talent. Because so many talented people fall by the wayside. In every writing program I was ever around as a student, I thought I was lucky to hang out with these people. I would be the last to guess that I was the one who was going to survive and they weren't. But for whatever reason, their dream became untenable to them. That's just a matter of character, and there's no way you can teach that.

AMY TAN

ROBERT FOOTHORAP

"I'm just as vulnerable to
rejection as any other writer."

*Admittedly, Amy Tan hasn't had much rejection in her writing
career. She was a freelance business writer when her first published
story landed her both an agent and a book contract. Her first novel,*
The Joy Luck Club, *went straight to the top of the* New York Times
*bestseller list. It was also a finalist for the National Book Award and
the National Book Critics Circle Award. Subsequent novels,* The
Kitchen God's Wife, The Hundred Secret Senses, *and* The
Bonesetter's Daughter, *made the bestseller lists as well. Tan has
also written two children's books, and her short fiction has
appeared frequently in the* Atlantic, Grand Street, Harper's, *and*
The New Yorker.

*Although she's been fortunate in her career, Tan says the fear of
rejection that was nurtured in childhood has never left her. In fact,
the more well-known she becomes, the greater her fears. She finds
reviews and criticism so unsettling that she refuses to read them,
and she suffers from anxiety and depression whenever a new book*

is published. Tan's happiest moments are when she's in her office writing, far out of the spotlight.

Tan was born in Oakland, California, in 1952 and lives in San Francisco.

Q: *When you were eight years old, you wrote an award-winning essay, "What the Library Means to Me." Since then, it seems, you've had nothing but success. Was there ever any point in your career when you were rejected as a writer?*

A: I didn't have great expectations that I would become a novelist. I didn't go through huge rejections—in part because I didn't try.

I had been doing business writing for quite a while, but it took me until I was thirty-five to try my hand at fiction writing. When I started writing fiction, my goal in life was to get something published in a nice literary magazine such as *Ploughshares* or *Grand Street*. I wasn't even looking at, say, *The New Yorker*.

Knowing that I certainly would get rejected, I would send my stories out. I thought I would have a collection of letters in this wonderful little format with the *New Yorker* at the top. I planned to pin them on my bulletin board and create a collage of sorts, to encourage me and to show that I had written these stories and sent them off into the world.

I *did* get rejection letters, but right from the beginning I got very nice rejection letters. One letter from the *New Yorker* said, "It didn't quite work for us, but we hope you will continue to send us your stories." And that was from an actual editor, hand-typed on a funny old typewriter! It was way more than I ever expected.

I got those kinds of rejection letters for about two years, and then I had a story accepted—not by the *New Yorker*, but by a very, very small literary magazine that later went out of business. That was because Molly Giles, a friend who is now my editor, had recommended me to them.

Q: *That magazine,* FM Five, *played a big role in your career.*

A: It's a great piece of hope, I think, when you realize how many writers had their beginnings with little magazines. Because that piece was then seen by editors at other magazines, and then by my agent. So it led to bigger things.

You can get read more easily if you've been published in a small magazine. When the magazines are well respected, people know that the editors have discerning taste. So I think they're a great venue for serious literary writers. And it just so, so rarely happens the other way—by sending it out to *The New Yorker*.

After that first story was published, an agent contacted me. She asked me to write one more story and an outline. Then she took that, unbeknownst to me, to New York, shopped it around and got five offers. I was so stunned that I thought this agent was some sort of flimflam person! I thought that she had presented work by some other writer and claimed it was mine.

That was the end of my shopping. That's very unusual, though. I was somebody who knew all along that it was going to take years. My goal, as I said, was to be published in a very decent little magazine when I was seventy.

Q: Have you saved your rejection letters from The New Yorker?
A: Yeah, I have them somewhere. I should take them out and make a little display. Because I always was going to do that with all the rejection letters.

Q: Well, you just don't have enough of them. That's the problem.
A: I know. But it's good to remind myself of those early days. To just say, "You're very, very lucky."

Q: So apart from The New Yorker, *which has since published you many times, you really haven't had much rejection in your life.*
A: In one way, I have lived with rejection. I think I grew up feeling quote "rejected" in the sense that my parents were so critical of things I did. This was really just their way of raising kids, but as a result I felt afraid to expect too much of myself. I think that's still true. I don't want to anticipate that I might win the lottery;

I don't want to anticipate that I might get a good review; I don't want to anticipate that somebody will read one of my books and like it. I'm afraid of people being sorely disappointed in things that I do.

But I didn't have a huge sense of disappointment when I got those early rejection letters, as in, "Oh my God, they didn't take my story? I can't believe it!" I had already moved on. And it never occurred to me that they truly would have *accepted* the story.

Q: So the key was keeping your expectations low?
A: My expectations were very low. Somebody asked me once what my goal was for my fiction, and I said, "I'm just doing it for myself. I'm finally doing something for myself." I had a business writing for everyone else, and that's what was paying the mortgage, and my clients were wonderful—but I had to find something for myself.

I thought it would take thirty or forty years to get published. I did! And I never wrote fiction with the idea that it would become a way of making a living. On the other hand, I didn't want to become a dilettante. I really applied myself to my craft—that was important to me. And the whole idea of sending the work out was necessary in my mind, to show that I did take it seriously.

Q: How did it feel to have that first story published?
A: I was thrilled. I had the letter framed, and I waited eagerly for the story to come out. I awaited the publication of that story more eagerly than I did, say, my first story published in *The New Yorker*. I was flabbergasted. And in a sense, I was a little disappointed—because this goal that I had to be published had happened so quickly. It was sort of like, now what am I going to do for the next thirty or forty years?

Q: Did you ever get any criticism of your work when you were first starting out?

A: I did read my work to my writers' group, which met once a week. Some people might consider that a form of opening yourself up to rejection or criticism. But I loved that process, for the most part. My adrenaline would be pumping, my voice would become shaky, and I would have a hard time reading my work out loud because it was so exciting. There, for the first time, I would receive a reaction of some sort from people.

There was never a time when people said, "This is perfect; you should have this published." There were always nitpicks about things, and there were also very large comments that had to do with why the story didn't work overall. To me, that was exciting. I would go back and redo the story and see what I had learned about the craft of writing a story. That was essentially how I wrote *The Joy Luck Club,* through this writers' group.

Q: How did you get involved with the writing group in the first place?

A: I went to a workshop at the Squaw Valley Community of Writers. It was the first writing workshop I had ever been to, where a professional writer and twelve other writers critiqued your manuscript. The comments I got there were such an eye-opener to me—issues of what is voice, what is story, which comes first, and how are they related.

I suddenly got a better focus on what my intentions might be as a writer. As I listened to feedback with these questions in mind, it gave me different ideas for assessing how well I had done. I found it to be a springboard for thinking about my writing. I also began to get a sense of myself as a writer, and I began to learn what to listen to and what not to listen to.

I think writing groups are very useful in helping you to develop self-editing skills. But beyond a certain point, you can get stuck in a rut. You can just going around and around, niggling over every single comma, and you never get through your book. So I found, after a while, that I needed to work on my own.

Q: Because you are famous, you know that whenever a new book comes out, it's going to have an audience. How does that affect your fear of rejection?

A: It makes my fear of rejection far greater. I had no idea of an audience when I wrote those early stories. I had some idea that people might read the rest of the stories, because they were part of *The Joy Luck Club.* But with the second book, *The Kitchen God's Wife,* I knew absolutely that people would be reading this book and reviewing it, and I was scared out of my mind. I broke three molars grinding my teeth at night, and I developed severe temporal mandibular joint pains, and back pains, and all kinds of tension-related disorders.

After *The Joy Luck Club* was published, I started a novel seven times. I would write two hundred pages and throw them away, write another two hundred pages and throw them away, because I was afraid to disappoint people. It was a terrible feeling. Most of the reviews of *The Joy Luck Club* had been terrific. So I said to myself, "What do they see? Why do they like it?" I was trying to figure out what that was and to imitate myself, if you can imagine!

Q: I have the reverse problem: I had a novel rejected and I'm trying to figure out what publishers didn't like. Both approaches are probably equally futile.

A: Absolutely. It took me such a long time to find a balance between writing and shutting out the rest of the world. That means I don't read any reviews of my books. It's part of the way I shut out the public sense of myself. I admit, it's ostrich-head-in-the-sand behavior, but I have to do it, because it's too nerve-wracking to think about them.

Q: Do your family and friends understand that they can't mention reviews?

A: They know! In fact, I do have to say, I'm probably just as vulnerable to rejection as any other writer. It's only my lack of awareness that keeps me shielded from that. I need that shielding because the expectations are so high, and because I am much more public than I used to be. There's a different sense now of what that rejection would mean.

Q: Does anyone ever slip up and break the rule?
A: I had a falling out with a friend who insisted on telling me terrible things that had been said about me. On top of that, I felt he did so with a certain sense of glee, which he insists that he didn't. But you know, a writer can be very fragile and interpret it quite differently. Talking to this person left me unable to write for days and days. So I decided I just couldn't see him anymore.

Q: Have you ever sat down and talked with a book critic who gave you a negative review?
A: Yes. Your critics are with you at every event that you go to. I was once at a party with my first editor. We were standing there and she said, "Oh, there's so-and-so, who just did a review of your book."

Before she could say anything more, I walked over to this woman, because I knew her, and I said, "Oh, hi, and by the way thanks for the review, it's really great and thank you so much!" And she just looked at me in this really bizarre way.

We talked for a little bit and then I came back to my editor. That's when she said, "Oh, by the way, it was a terrible review."

Q: Yes, but wasn't that the perfect way to put that reviewer in her place?
A: In hindsight!

Q: I think one thing people don't understand is that criticism means more to a writer than getting your ego hurt. It also affects your creative process.
A: Oh, absolutely! It affects my creative process in that I think that I'm not creative at all, and that I shouldn't be writing. I

think this is true especially for people who become more public, because you feel more personally insulted. You know that these critics know who you are, and that you've met them. When they write things that are very personal, you end up feeling assaulted.

Q: Have you ever been rejected by a relative for revealing family secrets?
A: The only person who was really upset was one of my uncles, who thought that a certain male character in one book was his father. His father, whom he adored, was also the man who had raped my grandmother, who later committed suicide. This man was not a great man in some respects, obviously, but he was apparently a good citizen and a good father.

In my book, this character did something that got him in trouble, and he was seen as a Japanese collaborator. Even though he is actually shown to have been falsely accused, my uncle got very upset with me. And you can't explain to people that some aspects of this character did match, but that not all of them did.

Now my uncle is no longer upset, in fact, he's been gathering his stories for me, and hoping I will use them.

Q: What do you think turned his thinking around?
A: I believe that he saw, after a while, that my books are not written out of revenge; that they are really written from a sense of pride and a desire to understand the family. He also saw that this character was not intended to be his father in all kinds of exact ways.

Now he wants to entrust his stories to me, which is very sweet. Whenever anybody does that, it's as though they're handing over the legacy of their life, and they want you to be the keeper. That's the strongest indication that he knew these things were not meant to be vindictive toward his side of the family.

In fact, that's true of most of my family. They want to tell me stories. They're hoping that I will incorporate them into my fiction. I think they also understand that I write with a sense of love, not with any vindictive motives.

Q: How did your mother react to The Joy Luck Club?

A: She was annoyed that people 'assumed everything was non-fiction—as if I didn't have the ability to make things up! She wanted people to recognize my writing as a talent, not just as dictation.

Most of my books are dedicated to my mother. My mother wanted certain stories told, particularly in the second book, *The Kitchen God's Wife.* When she saw I was struggling to start my second book, she said, "Why don't you write my true story?" I laughed and said, "That's not how fiction is done."

It wasn't until later that I realized that that is exactly how fiction *is* done. You find the most personal, heartfelt reason to write the story. And she gave me that reason. The reason was to listen finally to her story straight through, and to give it back to her in another version. Then she was able to see that I had finally understood what she went through, living in an abusive marriage and losing her children and things like that.

In the past my mother would obsess about things that had upset her and talk for hours and hours and hours, going over the same ground. I think she was always looking for me to make her feel that I understood and sympathized with her. After my mother read *The Joy Luck Club,* she started doing the same thing, but then she stopped and said, "I don't have to tell you. You understand." Because of the book, she knew that I *did* understand what she'd gone through.

So that was wonderful. Despite the fact of her saying, "I know these stories aren't true," she also knew that what *was* true was the heart of what I was feeling about our relationship. That's essentially what I wanted to capture. She sensed that it's much easier for me to capture what is emotionally true through the manipulations of fiction.

Q: There's some healing of family relationships that goes on through this process?

A: I don't set off to write to heal myself, necessarily, or to heal others. But I think that if you are a writer, you naturally come upon areas that open up tender points—deep, deep wounds—and areas in which you can find a sense of consolation and resolution. It's not that the whole thing happens each time that you write, and it's not as though you come to the task or the art of writing with those goals in mind. But they do happen organically, and you can't predict when they're going to happen.

By the same token you can open up a whole box of biting wasps that has had the lid on for a long time, and they can keep biting you for a long time!

Q: That's the other side of the coin.
A: Yes, exactly. So I've never been one to recommend writing literary fiction as a form of therapy. It may be that it naturally happens, and it may be that some people can write specifically to achieve that. It just is not so in my case.

Q: You have spoken before about your struggles with depression. Are your depression and your writing interrelated?
A: I don't think in periods of depression I'm able to write better. During times of depression I'm not able to write at all.

On the other hand, the things that cause the depression, are what, in part, fuel my writing later. It's very interesting to me how depression will cast your mind and your eyes into seeing the world in a completely different way. As a writer, one of the skills you have to have is to be able to cast yourself into different perspectives, and it does help me to see from a different vantage point.

I often wonder whether the depression is inherited, since my grandmother killed herself, and my mother was suicidal all her life. I also wonder if it was passed on through an emotional legacy, a sense of hopelessness or a bleakness, a sharp-eyedness toward things that are dangerous.

As the years go by, some of the qualities that have been passed on to me, either by DNA or by example and shaping, have evolved. I think my humor has increased over the years, but so has my fearfulness. Maybe the fear of rejection is greater, too. But who's to say that that is just a result of the natural atrophy of your muscles as you get old, or the reinforcement of the experience through being a more public author?

Q: Some writers think if only they were published, they would never be depressed. Yet that obviously is not the case with you.
A: No. My bouts of depression have always come on precisely the day that I was published. The very first time I was published I went into severe depression and could not stop crying. And every single time a book has come out, I have this terrible sense of dread. On the day of publication, I'm usually profoundly depressed.

Q: Do you have any idea why that is?
A: I think it relates to the fear that something will be taken away from me, and that I will no longer be myself anymore.

Q: You mean, because you're sending your little child into the world?
A: No, it's more that I'm going to be out in public again, subject to expectations that I'm not going to be able to meet. There's this terrible dread about that.

Q: All evidence to the contrary.
A: I don't know. I'm sure the reality is that I have been far luckier than many writers, but I believe that my reviews these days are probably half and half—half good, half bad.

Q: John Cleese was once asked in an interview whether being in therapy would make him lose his ability to be creative or funny anymore. He said something like, "I'd rather be healed than be creative."
A: I think that even if therapy worked for you and if you miraculously got rid of every single thing that caused you to be

depressed, that those origins of what had made you depressed would still be in your memory and you could still rely upon them. Your humor might have different takes on those past pains, but—and I'm going back to the biting wasp metaphor—I think there will always be new nests of biting insects that can add to your repository of humor tools when you need them.

Q: *So it's not a big worry.*
A: I don't think so.

Q: *If you had never been published at this point in you life, would you still be writing?*
A: I would be definitely be writing business things to keep food on the table. I actually had a very lucrative freelance business, and I was quite comfortable. But I was very unhappy with what I was writing, because it wasn't important to me.

I know now that I needed to find expression of my own passions and ideas. There are things I can't articulate out loud. I don't even know how I feel until I work it out on the page, and sometimes it helps me most to work it out in the form of an image. If I were not writing fiction, I think I would be drawing, or doing something else in the way of individual, personal expression.

Q: *Have you ever been in a position to reject work by other writers?*
A: I once did a workshop in which I critiqued two people's manuscripts. I gave them both good comments, and comments of puzzlement. So, for example, I'd say, "This is an intriguing opening," and then maybe later I'd say, "I'm still expecting to hear more about so and so," or, "I haven't heard about so-and-so who was so intriguing at the beginning." It wasn't things like, "This is terrible," or "This is wonderful." It was things having to do with voice and story. I provided what had always been given to me, and which I'd always found very helpful, which is the comments of a reader.

I realized, however, that because of my being so well published, the people whose manuscripts I critiqued were really hoping that I would say, "Here's the card of an agent, this is going to become a bestseller." Any other comment was devastating to them. They saw the pages marked up—I'd spent hours on them—and their faces fell. Even though I assured them that I was doing what had always been done for me. None of that helped.

Q: So your critique was rejected!
A: My comments as a reader were *totally* rejected. And I was rejected as a person who could possibly help them, because I didn't say, "You are the next Thomas Pynchon, where have you been?"

After that experience, I gave up commenting on people's work. I won't do reviews, either. And I would never accept a position where I could do any kind of harm to another writer.

Q: I'm sure that when you were a corporate writer, you had plenty of experience with feedback and criticism.
A: Right. And I don't suppose I would mind book reviews that were critical if they were done in a literary manner.

I read reviews of other writers from time to time, and I'm amazed at how often I see the kind of personal review that is attacking writers for the length of their eyelashes. I want to shake them, and say, "Why don't we get back to the realm of literary criticism? Save the personal realm for the interview. Don't do it here!" But this is all too often what happens now in reviews. It's as if the reviewer is taking glee in how clever he or she is at berating the writer.

Q: What kind of advice do you give writer friends about dealing with rejection?
A: First of all, I tell them not to read reviews, especially if they're trying to write another book.

I also advise them to try to go back to that place where you first wanted to write, or the first moment that you had that epiphany of what writing is about, and try to recapture that. Write down what is important to you about the writing and just focus on that. That's what I try to do. It's not as easy as it sounds!

The other thing is to just simply sit down and write a page a day. Just do it like an assignment to get the whole process of writing going, because often in doing that you tumble again into that space that is private and wonderful and creative...

Q: ... *and where no one can hurt you.*
A: Yes. I think that's the reason why my writing space is like a cubbyhole. I actually am in a former closet. It's dark and it's crammed full of little things and there are no windows. It's small and private and I'm the only one in it.

EDMUND WHITE

"Don't allow yourself to suffer even for
five minutes over a rejection."

*Talk about braving rejection—try getting published as a gay writer
in the United States in the 1960s. Edmund White tried and failed
many times. Then his luck turned in 1973, when his novel*
Forgetting Elena *was published and Vladimir Nabokov publicly
called it his "favorite American novel." Today White is an author,
teacher, and editor esteemed on both sides of the Atlantic. His honors include a Guggenheim Fellowship, the French Government's
Officier de L'Ordre des Arts et Lettres, a National Book Critics
Circle Award, and membership in the American Academy of Arts
and Letters. White has taught at Johns Hopkins, Columbia, Brown,
and Yale universities and is presently a professor of creative writing
at Princeton.*

*White was born in 1940 in Cincinnati. In the mid-sixties he
moved to New York City and pursued a career in publishing at*
Time-Life Books, Saturday Review, *and* Horizon. *Among his novels, memoirs, and biographies are* A Boy's Own Story, Genet: A

Biography, The Farewell Symphony, Marcel Proust, The Married Man, The Flaneur: A Stroll through the Paradoxes of Paris, *and* Art and Letters. *He has also edited anthologies, including* Loss Within Loss: Artists in the Age of AIDS.

Q: Your early career was difficult, to say the least. How did you handle rejection when you were first starting out?
A: I took rejection really hard. My entire sense of self was tied up in the idea of acceptance, because I was gay in a period when you weren't supposed to be gay. In other words, if you grew up in the forties and fifties, homosexuality could only be viewed as a crime or a sin or a mental illness.

Q: Or maybe all three!
A: Or maybe all three. And writing, for me, counted as a way of redeeming this terribly shoddy experience and turning this dross into gold. If I couldn't get accepted and I couldn't get a book published, it was as though not only was I a bad person, but I had no redeeming product to show for it.

I never wanted to be rich and I never particularly wanted to be famous. What I *really* wanted was to be published. I wanted this object to exist as a kind of proof that everything I'd ever been through didn't count for nothing. And I always wrote very close to my own experience.

Q: Did you have a hard time finding an agent?
A: I happened to get an agent early on through some college friends. That was lucky—but she wasn't able to sell my books. She submitted three novels to many, many, many publishers and they were all rejected.

Q: How did the fact that your subject matter was homosexual play into your difficulty in getting your work published?
A: Well, I'm talking about submitting stuff in 1965, 1966, 1967—and gay liberation didn't begin until 1969.

Q: *Did people admit that it was the content of your books that made them turn you down?*

A: There was a lot of what you could call displacement. If you're writing about something like integration or gay liberation or feminism in an era before those things are accepted, middle-class editors are too clever to say that that's what bothers them. They displace their irritation onto other things.

Years later, I met these editors. Some of them told me that they themselves were gay. Though they had liked my book, they didn't dare speak out for it in an editorial meeting, because that might lead people to think that *they* were gay. For instance, one of the editors who rejected my writing was a guy who went on to win the Pulitzer Prize as a journalist, and who became a good friend years later. But he never mentioned the theme, which was the troublesome thing, in the rejection letter.

I'm not saying that my writing was perfect at that period, or is now. But it certainly was slightly better than the run-of-the-mill—and yet I could never get anything published. Meanwhile, I had a very good straight friend who was exactly my age, and who worked where I worked, at Time/Life Books. He had three books published by the time he was thirty. They were sort of Pynchonesque comedies with, of course, bona fide heterosexual content. So, no problem.

Q: *So your straight colleague beat you to the punch. But has anyone heard of this person today?*

A: No. But you don't *know* that when you're in your twenties. And I would suffer terribly!

I remember really being jerked around by a certain editor at Knopf who was famous for making quick and resolute decisions. But he kept my manuscript for a year, and then he called me in and said he said he was "dickering" with the idea, but he couldn't make up his mind. He said, "Well, I don't think I'm going to do it, because I like junk, and this isn't really junk." Later, when

I was living in Rome, he finally decided against it and my agent sent me the rejection letter.

. Much later this editor and I became friendly acquaintances, because I don't like to hold a grudge—but that was the most painful rejection I ever had.

Q: So your book wasn't junky enough, that's why he didn't want it?
A: I really was puzzled by it all. And then, what finally happened is that Richard Howard, bless his heart, came along. He was a Pulitzer Prize-winning poet and a translator and a very energetic and generous literary figure, who was openly gay before almost anybody else. He read what's now called my first novel, *Forgetting Elena,* and he counseled me on how to restructure it, which I did. Then he resubmitted it to Random House, which had already rejected it, along with twenty-two other publishers.

Forgetting Elena was published in 1973. Three years after it was published, Nabokov said in *Esquire* that it was his favorite American novel. So even though it never sold more than a thousand copies, it nevertheless had a cult status because of that.

Q: Even though the content was gay?
A: *Forgetting Elena* was gay only in the most oblique way. It was an allegory, or a mystery, or a fantasy—but it was not a realistic novel and it certainly wasn't about gays running around on Fire Island. It was about a prince in an island kingdom who had amnesia. It even had two long heterosexual sex scenes.

So what's interesting is, the first book that got published wasn't gay, even though I had been writing explicitly gay books before that. My own feeling is that people in the sixties could accept homosexual content only if it was about very marginal people, whether it was Jean Genet's *Our Lady of the Flowers* or Hubert Selby's *Last Exit to Brooklyn* or William Burroughs' *Naked Lunch.* All of these books were acceptable because they were clearly about people *not* like you and me.

They were about transvestites and prostitutes and drug addicts and weirdoes.

Whereas I was writing about the guy in the office next to yours, who wore a suit and tie, who you didn't know was gay, and who even brought girls to office parties, but who would rush home at night and put on his jeans and go to a back-room bar. This was disturbing to people, especially to all those closeted gays who were editors.

Q: People wanted homosexuality to be exotic.
A: That's right. Exotic was okay, familiar was not. Because it was too close for comfort. And I think, to this day, that straights would rather watch drag queens walking down the street than nicely dressed middle-class gays.

But back to rejection: I took it so deeply and so painfully! I even contemplated suicide several times. When Knopf finally decided not to take that first novel in 1970 and I got the letter from my agent, I was living in Rome. I remember thinking, "I'm going to commit suicide unless God sends me a sign." I sat down on a bench by the Forum, and I was sobbing, and a man came over—a handsome, big, tall Dutch man—and put his arm around my shoulders and said, "What's wrong, young man?" And I said, "OK, that's a sign from God. I don't have to commit suicide." But it really was that bad.

You put all of your money on one card and if it doesn't come up, then you feel as if you've failed in some massive way. And I do think there was this other aspect of trying to redeem myself and, at the same time, forge a sexual identity.

People had all these terribly pejorative views of homosexuality—including homosexuals themselves. It was only in 1969 with Stonewall and the beginning of gay liberation, that people began to think that homosexuality might be a group that was value-free—as good as, no better than, other groups. But that was brand-new at the time. And I feel like I always was part of that movement, so it made my case very special.

Q: You were quite the renegade.

A: In the late 1970s, *Harper's Queen,* an English magazine, called me "the most maligned man in America," which I was quite proud of. But what happens is that things switch very quickly, and you suddenly become successful and popular, or at least esteemed, by a small group of readers. And then, people who weren't around in the early days assume you were always that way. They assume that, in fact, you're a member of the Establishment. So you go from being a pariah to being a member of the Establishment with no transition.

Q: And you're probably reviled in both situations, but for different reasons.

A: Exactly. But anyway I'd much rather be a member of the Establishment than a pariah, and I've known both.

Q: How much time did you spend getting rejected before you finally got published?

A: I finished my first novel when I was fourteen, another when I was eighteen, another one when I was twenty, another one when I was twenty-two. The one I wrote when I was twenty-two I submitted, and the one I wrote when I was twenty-five I submitted, and it was not until I was thirty-three that I finally got something published. It was a good, long way.

Q: But it sounds like you were convinced from the very beginning that this was what you wanted to do.

A: I had a real strong sense of destiny. Unfortunately reality wasn't cooperating. Also, I don't think I was a good, steady, mature, hard worker. I felt the world owed me instant recognition, and so I was angry all the time that I wasn't getting it. But it wasn't as though I was writing stuff that was easy to sell. I never for a minute wanted to win on *their* terms, I only wanted to win on *my* terms. I don't know how I got such a feeling of entitlement!

Q: You weren't willing to cut the world any slack.
A: No! I was angry and demanding and wounded and very, very unhappy. I really was deeply unhappy throughout my teens and twenties, and I really only started getting happy towards my mid-thirties.

Q: And that coincides with publication.
A: Yes! To this day, I'm very insecure as a writer and as a person. I always expect the worst to happen. I immediately go into a tailspin if editors even have a few questions about my latest manuscript.

I think it's I just because I went through too much. Another person in my situation would have accepted the rejections as a challenge, and been convinced that he was talented, and kept going. Which I *did* do, but I did it with ill grace.

Q: You really are very hard on yourself.
A: It's the truth.

Q: Do you still have a hard time dealing with rejection?
A: Oh, yeah. I get very angry. Even editorial suggestions sometimes make me upset. But I don't want to over-paint that. I just finished following the suggestions of an editor in England who I trust absolutely, who wanted me to cut one-fourth of my book, and to make hundreds and hundreds of little changes. But if I feel that somebody has shoddy motives—that is, that they want my work to be more "commercial," or they haven't been paying attention, or they are trying to force their message onto it—that infuriates me.

Q: Do you think young writers have a harder time starting out now than when you did?
A: I was talking to Don DeLillo about this. He said, "You know, the thing about these poor students starting off now is that their first book has to make it big. There used to be a thing called

'promise,' and a publisher would be committed to you. They would nurture you through two or three books that didn't do so well until you finally fulfilled your promise—or didn't. But now, you have to hit it big with your first book or your career's finished."

I think something similar to that is true of tons of mid-list writers who are friends of mine, or myself. I feel you can easily screw up two or three times in a row and have tiny sales and bad reviews and then—oops!—you're off the map.

Q: As an established writer, do you still get rejected because you write about gay subjects?
A: Yes. Here's an example. I just came back from Michigan, where I was invited to speak at my old prep school, Cranbrook. I was the last of my class who was in any way distinguished to be invited, but I did finally get invited. Then, at the last minute, they tried to un-invite me. They called up in a total panic and said, "We must know precisely what you're going to discuss."

I refused to let them look at what I was going to say in advance. I said, "I'll just drop out if it's too much of a problem." Then, when I got there, I found out that they had printed up a chapter of *A Boy's Own Story* that was about the school, but they had suppressed several passages of it.

Censorship still reigns, and homosexuality is still a problem for a lot of people.

Q: You've written biographies of Jean Genet and Marcel Proust. Have you learned anything about how these writers have handled rejection?
A: Genet actually didn't have any rejections. He had a meteoric rise, and he became a national treasure by the time he was forty-two. Proust *did* have a lot of rejection, but he had a totally Olympian, convinced calm about his genius from the very beginning. So they really weren't of much use to me.

I mean, Proust eventually paid to have *Swann's Way*, the first volume of his book, published. He had submitted it to several commercial publishers, but they all rejected it. So then he just went on to pay for it. His first book did very, very well and got lots of attention. Then right after the First World War, he published the second volume, which won the Goncourt prize, the best prize you can get in France. By the time his third book was out, he was awarded the Legion of Honor.

Proust definitely "made it" in French terms, although it wasn't until after his death that he got international acclaim. But he always knew that he was immortal. He knew that very early on. He was convinced of it.

Q: Proust is supposed to have tied special knots around the manuscript of Remembrance of Things Past *to see if it had actually been read by editors.*
A: What happened was, it was submitted to Gallimard, which was then called the Nouvelle Revue Française. And André Gide, who was the head of the reader's committee, looked down on Proust because he thought of him as a society writer. Proust had written a gossip column for *Le Figaro* and was sort of a dancing master type, running around and being a capon to duchesses. So serious writers looked down on him, just as they would today. I mean, let's say, the gossip columnist William Norwich wrote a novel. I don't think anyone would really take it seriously. And if he turned out to be the Don DeLillo of his generation, people would be very surprised.

Q: So you don't look to Proust for inspiration when you're having doubts about your own writing?
A: In one way, yes, because I think he had a very long-range vision of his career. But the biggest encouragement I had when I was starting out was from Marilyn Schaefer, who I met when I was first starting out and is still my best friend.

Marilyn was a painter, and she always had this very long-range view of what a career was—that you'd go through your apprentice years and then have your years of maturity. You weren't supposed to be an overnight success, you were supposed to build a career. I was fourteen when I met Marilyn, and she was twenty, I think. She really inspired me a lot.

Q: *Do you think her insight was based on the fact that she had a painter's perspective, as opposed to a writer's?*
A: Maybe. Because painters tend to flourish in their old age.

Q: *And they also expect to go through a long period of training.*
A: Exactly. It's more of a workshop approach.

Q: *How do you advise friends or students who are dealing with rejection?*
A: One thing is that you should keep as many balls in the air as possible. If you're sending out short stories, you should make up twenty envelopes and send them all out at once. Or, if you don't think that's cricket, have them all ready so that when the thing comes back, you just flip it into the next envelope. It should be purely mechanical.

I was once an editor at *Saturday Review,* and I had to choose poems for that magazine. So I know about the exigencies of editing—that either you're too busy to read the stuff, or you have such a backlog that you don't need any more, or you want something funny, or you want something seasonal, or you want something by somebody famous. There are all these stupid considerations. So when a young writer treats an editor like he's the guardian of Mount Parnassus, and assumes that that editor has actually seen through to the heart of the work and found it wanting, this is such a foolish notion of what editors really do!

I mean, editors are lazy like everybody else, they're disorganized like everybody else, they're influenced by the latest craze like everybody else, and they're more likely to help their friends than other people—just like everybody else.

Q: I assume the same thing applies to book reviewers?
A: Here's a good example. I remember meeting Edith Oliver, who at that time was in charge of book reviews at the *The New Yorker*. My first novel, *Forgetting Elena*, got very few reviews, but I kept hearing that it was going to get a positive review in *The New Yorker*. Finally I met Edith Oliver at a party, and I said, "Whatever happened to that review of *Forgetting Elena*?"

She said, "Well, you know, my best friend is Edmund Wilson, so he has your first name; and his wife Elena had just died. When I saw the combination of those two names, you understand, it was impossible for me to run a review."

Q: Talk about capricious!
A: Well, that's it. Everyone is so capricious! Once you live in New York and you meet all these people whose rejections you wept over, you realize that half of them are so boring and stupid that you wouldn't even cross the room to talk to them. But it just goes to show how insecure we all are, that we are quick to make these father transferences or mother transferences onto all these so-called authorities.

Q: Yes, but these people also have the power to make or break your career.
A: Of course. But you should see them as something to be out-witted, rather than as the ultimate judgment by God. I think a little bit of scorn for your enemies is good. Send things out as frequently as you can, and just realize it's a numbers game. And don't allow yourself to suffer even for five minutes over a rejection. Not that we can ever really *do* this!

WILLIAM ZINSSER

THOMAS VINCENT

"Your obligation to yourself is to
get the damn thing back in the mail."

*Although William Zinsser already had thirty years of experience as
a journalist and author under his belt, he says it wasn't until he
wrote* On Writing Well: An Informal Guide to Writing
Nonfiction *that he found his true voice. Since then,* On Writing
Well *has become beloved of teachers and students alike and has
sold more than one million copies. In his books and classes, Zinsser
encourages writers to focus on their own values instead of on pleasing editors and publishers.*

*Zinsser was born in New York City in 1922. He began his
career in 1946 at the* New York Herald Tribune, *where he wrote
feature articles, drama and film criticism, and editorials. As a
freelance writer, he wrote for* Look, Life, The New Yorker, *and
the* New York Times. *He taught writing at Yale for nine years and
was executive editor at Book-of-the-Month Club for eight years.
His books include* Mitchell and Ruff: An American Profile,
Writing to Learn, Spring Training, *and* Writing About Your

Life: A Journey into the Past. *He has edited several books about writing, including* Going on Faith: Writing As a Spiritual Quest *and* Inventing the Truth: The Art and Craft of Memoir. *He lives in New York City.*

Q: *You said that rejection has not been important in your career. Why?*
A: My first job was as a journalist with the *New York Herald Tribune*. They employed me for thirteen years, so there was no rejection there. When I left the *Herald Tribune* in 1959 to become a freelance writer, my name was already out there. It was not as hard for me as it would have been for people starting cold.

I supported myself as a freelance writer from 1959 to 1970, when I went to Yale [to teach]. For the last five of those years, I had an annual contract with *Life*. They didn't have to renew it each year, so there was always an element of risk there. And before I started to work for *Life,* there were five or six years when I was just sitting at home and supporting my family as a freelance writer. I was doing a lot of writing and sending it out in the mail. Those were the main years of risk, 1959–1967.

Q: *Any advice for the rest of us freelancers?*
A: The one thing I could say that might be useful is, whenever I sent something out and it came back, I didn't waste any time crying over the fact that it had come back. I made it a principle to get it back in the mail by noon.

Q: *What time was your mail delivered?*
A: Around ten in the morning.

Q: *That didn't give you much time!*
A: Well you don't *need* much time. You've got to get it back in circulation. You can waste a lot of time on self-pity, and self-pity has no part in being a successful freelance writer. Nor does indulging yourself by thinking about how stupid editors were

for not seeing what a wonderful thing you've written. Because I really don't think editors know what they want. I think they're basically timorous people.

Q: *And you speak as an editor as well as a writer!*
A: Yes. I've been an editor for a long time.

Editors don't really know what they want until they see it. And different editors at the same magazine have different opinions, which is why you get all those terrible letters that say, "Several of us here thought it was wonderful, but finally the general opinion was that it was just not right for us." Which means that on any one magazine, if there are three or four editors making a decision, half of them may like it and half of them may not, and finally they say, "It's not right for us."

It doesn't do any good to think about what's going through their heads. They are just an impersonal agency of fate that you have to deal with. You can't afford to waste any time on who they are or why they didn't appreciate your work.

Your obligation to yourself is to get the damn thing back in the mail. You write a new cover letter, you put the stamps on it, you take it out to the mailbox, you put it in, and you forget about it.

Q: *It seems as if all publications make their decisions by committee these days.*
A: The *New York Times Magazine* has something like eleven different editors. When you deal with the articles editor you think he's in charge of articles. You send a piece in, and he says, "Well, the deputy assistant Sunday editor said it might be okay, but when he handed it up to the assistant Sunday editor, he felt we had done something like that three years ago and we couldn't repeat it."

You finally realize you're not really dealing with the articles editor; you're dealing with a whole cabal of people who have their own opinions. And they don't finally even know what they want.

I wrote a piece that ran in a very good magazine a year or two ago, and the editor, who was a senior editor, said "It's a wonderful piece, and I'm sure we'll take it." Then, of course, he had to show it to the editor, who was out of town for the next three weeks. There's no sense fretting about all this. It's just built into the system.

Q: Do you ever get upset when a piece is rejected?
A: I try not to let that kind of thing bother me, because there's nothing I can do about it. However, I think the worst thing that happens to freelance people—not only writers, but painters and artists and musicians—is that they are made the victims of situations that are not their fault. By which I mean, when you ask to get paid, they say, "The accounting office has moved to Topeka." Or, "The person you're dealing with is on maternity leave." Or, "Our new vice president hasn't come on board yet." Or, "We're undergoing a redesign." Or, "It has to be vetted by our lawyers and there's a big backlog."

What I finally say to them, which I think is very liberating, is, "That's *your* problem. If you have a backup of lawyers, hire more lawyers. The fact that the accounting office is in Topeka doesn't matter, because that's what we have telecommunications for. If the person I was dealing with is on maternity leave, that's not my problem. Get somebody to replace her and read my manuscript."

I think it's scandalous that so many magazines and publishers use their own inefficiency and ineptitude as excuses for why they can't deal with their writers.

Q: Is that true of book publishing as well as magazine publishing?
A: God, yes! There's nobody home in the publishing industry. You can't get those people on the phone. They're at the pre-sales conference, or they're at the sales conference, or they're at the post-sales conference, or they're at the Frankfurt Book Fair. They don't get back to you for months. And there's no excuse for that. It's a basic discourtesy.

Q: Has this been the case throughout your career, or is it getting worse?

A: I touch on this in the last chapter of *On Writing Well*. I think it's gotten worse because the younger generations of editors regard courtesy as a frill. Courtesy is not a frill; it's a professional obligation. It's organic to the craft.

Editors are thoughtless about the emotional and financial needs of freelance people. The writer writes a piece, and of course the writer is dying until he or she hears whether the piece has been accepted. The writer is entitled to know within a decent amount of time whether it's acceptable or not. The writer should also know when he's going to get paid without having to keep calling.

Now in saying all this, I realize I'm just kvetching. But in fact, although I've never been a member of The Authors' League or the Authors' Guild, or any of those groups, I regard myself as a one-man unguided missile. I've written letters to publishers and editors, trying to get them to behave better—not on my behalf, because I'm not waiting for the check by the mailbox, but on behalf of all the younger writers who don't dare challenge the authorities.

We have to speak up for ourselves against these callousnesses of behavior. Telling writers they can't handle your work because of internal problems, is meretricious. Clean up your house! If you have "publisher" on your letterhead, publish the book! Or reject it—promptly.

Writers are providing the material for these people who claim they're publishing, and they're doing it as honorably as they can. But they don't have any income stream. And all these people who are claiming "We can't talk to you," are getting their paychecks every two weeks.

Q: After all these years, do you still wait by the phone after you send a piece out?

A: Yes, and it's an extremely naïve thing to do. You *can't* wait by the phone. Editors are going to come and go forever in your life, and they're all going to have agendas of their own, and they're all going to be subject to all kinds of unforeseen corporate decisions.

The publishing industry today is so volatile that there is no way a freelance writer sitting at his desk can even begin to predict the concatenation of forces that are working on these people to keep them from making any kind of decision. It's entirely wasted energy.

Editors come and go, but you, the writer, are stuck with yourself for the rest of your writing life. So be true to your own values and don't try to imagine what editors will want, what publishers will want, what agents will want. You will always write your best if you write for yourself.

Q: Given all this, do you advise students to pursue a career in writing?
A: I don't really let the question come up, and the reason I don't is that I'm not trying to teach people how to sell; I'm trying to teach them how to write. There's a big difference.

When I first started teaching my course, "People and Places," at The New School in the early 1990s, students would come up to me and say, "You know, Mr. Zinsser, this is the only writing course I've ever taken that isn't market-driven." What a pathetic thing to say! But most people take writing courses because they want to learn how to sell what they write. I don't want to teach them how to sell; I want to teach them how to write. Because if they get their values right about writing, then their stuff will sell, in the long run. You just have to write out of your own values and hope that you're going to hit some editor who connects with them.

But it all comes back, really, to not weeping and complaining about the pieces that come back. That's just wasted energy.

Q: Why are writers more prone to weeping and complaining than members of other professions?
A: Because writing comes out of our selves. Most people are

extremely self-conscious about anything they write. We don't want anyone looking over our shoulder when we write a laundry list, because it's a piece of ourselves that we are putting on paper.

Writing is not only solitary, but we do so much of it in our heads even when we're not writing. A sentence that you can't disentangle, you're still trying to disentangle it when you're walking to the supermarket. You're living with your own work, and when you finally get it done right—you hope—you're sending a very painfully created piece of yourself out into the world. If somebody doesn't like it, you think that's the worst thing in the world.

Which brings me to another point. I can't teach someone who thinks that a rejection of his or her writing is a rejection of him or herself. It's not. Many editors and teachers have students they very much like and admire, but they are faced with the fact that they have to say, "That piece doesn't work. It's not good enough." At which point the writer bursts into tears. That does-n't do anybody any good, and it's not pertinent. The writer thinks, "He doesn't like my piece, therefore he doesn't like me. I am a terrible person." You're not a terrible person. You've just written something that doesn't work.

Q: Maybe that's because a lot of people are raised to believe that writing has to come out perfectly the first time.
A: If people are raised with that, they should get de-raised. *No* sentences come out right the first time. I rewrite and rewrite and rewrite and rewrite. Writing is very hard work and rewriting is the essence of writing. Sometimes it's elevated to an art; but basically it's a craft.

Q: Is there a difference between how you evaluate nonfiction versus fiction?
A: The nonfiction writer is infinitely accountable—to the truth, to the facts, to the person she interviewed, to the place she wrote about, and also to the craft—to not losing the

reader, and not confusing the reader, and all of that. With nonfiction we have the right to say, "That isn't interesting, that's boring, you haven't got that thing right," because we're dealing with the world of fact. We have no right to say that to the fiction writer. The fiction writer has made up his story between his own ears, and he or she is entitled to do that. Some of the really surprising successes in fiction writing are books like *Zen and the Art of Motorcycle Maintenance* or *Catch-22,* which are really far-out conceits.

Q: Which goes back to what you said about editors not knowing what they want.
A: Yes. If you had been Robert Pirsig and you had gone to an editor and said, "I want to write a book about motorcycling across the country with my twelve-year old son, and about my own flights in and out of delusion and psychosis between here and California," they would have said, "Get out of here." But if a work is true to a person's own character and vision and values, the editors—when they see it—are probably going to say, "This is an original piece of work." And it will sell.

I think fiction writers are more justifiably prone to the feeling that editors don't understand them, because theirs is a very personal vision. The nonfiction writer who is rejected has to realize that it has been to a great extent a failure of craft rather than a failure of editors to understand your vision.

Q: When you teach writing, you focus on the process rather than the finished result.
A: One of the most injurious forces in writing is people visualizing their beautiful, finished product before they even start. I want to wrest people away from this fixation on the finished product, because the act of writing is going to change their original conception. It's not going to be what they visualize. I am trying to get people to trust the process and not visualize the product. If the process is right, the product will take care of itself.

Q: You talk about this often in On Writing Well. *Did you ever imagine that book would strike such a chord with writers or would-be writers?*

A: No, because I had never written anything like it before. It was the first teaching book I'd ever written.

I think one reason people like the book is that people don't think they're hearing from a professor. They're hearing from another writer who is still continuing to struggle with his craft. Each edition of *On Writing Well* has new material consisting of things I learned since the previous edition—not by reading about writing, but by writing, and by continuing to practice the craft and set myself new challenges. I am not hiding from anybody in that book. I am very available.

Q: Which is what people respond to.

A: I think it is. When I first wrote the book I was trying to take the course I taught at Yale and put it down on paper. As I was writing it I occasionally thought of things that had been helpful to me in my own writing career. However, I told myself, "That's a little too personal, I shouldn't really say that." Because WASPs are taught not to make a public display of themselves. But finally I put them in anyway, and those were the things people responded to.

I had written a hell of a lot before this book came out. I wrote for the *Herald Tribune* for thirteen years and then for magazines like *The Saturday Evening Post.* I had a definite style that was modeled quite a bit on E. B. White's style—you know, casual, disarming, pseudo-charming, slightly humorous. But it was probably a somewhat contrived style. Then I wrote humor pieces for *Life* for five years in which I didn't use my voice at all; I was writing formula parody.

Finally, after five years of doing that, *Life* called up and said, "Whatever's in your typewriter, send it to somebody else, because we're closing." It was a day of national mourning. And I thought, "Hey, I'm off the hook!" I didn't mind that news one bit. I was exhausted from trying to be someone I wasn't.

Midway through my ten years at Yale I wrote *On Writing Well*, and I was writing for the first time as a teacher. I had no agenda except to be helpful. "This is who I am, I think I can help you, come along with me." I don't think my style was completely integrated with my character until I wrote that book.

Q: That's amazing! When was this?
A: That book came out in 1976, and I was born in 1922. So you can figure out how old I was when I finally found my true style, even though I had been writing all my life.

I didn't know when I was writing that book that it was going to have the effect it did. Which is why I have to believe that you're never going to write really well if you're trying to think: What do editors want? What do readers want? What do publishers want? You have to write, finally, for yourself. You have to go back to that word processor and write what you want to write.

Which is not to say it doesn't have to be craftsmanlike. You have to learn the craft, you have to not lose the reader, you have to construct it well, you have to cut, you have to think, you have to make a thousand learning-the-craft decisions.

Q: What's amazing to me is what a long process it is, to find your own style and your own voice.
A: It is! I think the thing that gives me the most satisfaction is not writing, but teaching. I really think of myself, first of all, as a teacher. Even my books that are ostensibly about something else are books about teaching and learning. That's my subject. It's only natural that my teacher's style is the style that most reflects who I am.

I'm a gregarious person. and I have a need for people. For years and years I sat alone at the bloody typewriter, making a living to support myself and my family. But I don't think the person who was sitting at that typewriter was all that interesting a person. A more interesting person is someone who makes himself available to other people and who becomes involved with other people. So it's no accident that the style that most reflects who I am didn't emerge until I wrote my first book as a teacher.

Which is another way of saying, there is no timetable. Give it time! And write what you want to write.

About the Author

CHRIS RAMIREZ

Aᴸᴛʜᴏᴜɢʜ ʜᴇʀ ᴡʀɪᴛɪɴɢ ʟɪꜰᴇ has had plenty of ups and downs, Catherine Wald has seen her work published in *Reader's Digest, Writer's Digest, Woman's Day,* the *New York Times, Poets & Writers,* and *Chicago Tribune,* among others. She has received fellowships and awards from the Ragdale Foundation, *Writer's Digest,* Women in Communications, and the International Association of Business Communicators. Her work has been anthologized in *The Essay Writer at Work* (Heinemann, 1998) and in *The Practical Writer* (Penguin Books, 2004). Her translation from the French of Valery Larbaud's 1912 *Childish Things* was published by Sun & Moon in 1994.

Wald's intimate knowledge of rejection began when an early poem was turned down by her high school literary magazine. As creator of www.rejectioncollection.com, the writer's and artist's online source for misery, commiseration, and inspiration, she has built her "rejexpertise" while spurring countless writers on to persistence and publication. She's also a lecturer and workshop leader on writing-related subjects.

Catherine Wald lives in Westchester County, New York, with her husband (a science teacher), her teenaged son and daughter, a dog, and two cats.